THE STORY
OF Jesus

Resources for *The Story*

Books

The Story

The Story for Teens

The Story for Kids

The Story for Children, a Storybook Bible

The Heart of the Story (by Randy Frazee)

Exploring the Story (by Adam Barr)

Curriculum

The Story Adult Curriculum Participant's Guide and DVD

The Story Teen Curriculum DVD

The Story of Jesus Teen Curriculum DVD

The Story Elementary Curriculum CD-ROM

The Story Early Elementary Curriculum CD-ROM

The Story Preschool CurriculumCD-ROM

The Story of Jesus Kids Curriculum

Other

The Story Implementation Guide

The Story Church Resource DVD

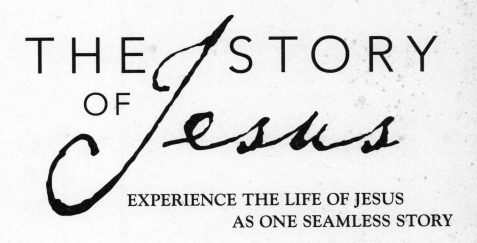

THE STORY OF *Jesus*

EXPERIENCE THE LIFE OF JESUS
AS ONE SEAMLESS STORY

RANDY FRAZEE

with Kevin and Sherry Harney

ADULT SMALL GROUP BIBLE STUDY

ZONDERVAN®

ZONDERVAN.com/
AUTHORTRACKER
follow your favorite authors

ZONDERVAN

The Story of Jesus Participant's Guide

The Story Adult Curriculum Participant's Guide
Copyright © 2011 by Randy Frazee

This title is also available as a Zondervan ebook.
Visit www.zondervan.com/ebooks.

Requests for information should be addressed to:

Zondervan, *Grand Rapids, Michigan 49530*

ISBN 978-0-310-69662-9

Interior design: Beth Shagene

Printed in the United States of America

13 14 15 16 17 18 19 20 /DCI/ 22 21 20 19 18 17 16 15 14 13 12 11 10 9 8 7 6 5 4 3 2 1

Contents

Introduction

SINCE 2005, WHEN *THE STORY* WAS FIRST PUBLISHED, HUNDREDS OF thousands of people have experienced God's great love affair with humanity through this accessible, chronologically arranged bestselling Bible. And whole families and churches around the world joined them when a complementary 31-session, children-through-adult curriculum was introduced in 2011.

Now, the seven sessions focused on the life of Jesus, complete with the corollary Bible readings from *The Story*, have been excerpted into a perfect study for small groups, churches, or individuals — designed for use with *The Story of Jesus* video, featuring the compelling teaching of pastor and author Randy Frazee.

Using This Participant's Guide

- Each session of this book consists of a Bible Reading (the related "chapter" of *The Story*) followed by a study guide that includes space for taking notes while viewing the video teaching, group discussion questions, prayer cues, and personal application ideas for between meetings.

- If you are unfamiliar with *The Story*, it features the words of the Bible as recorded in the New International Version (NIV). These portions of Scripture have been thoughtfully and carefully excerpted and then placed in chronological order. Transitions, which appear in italic, summarize omitted Scripture text in order to help the storyline read smoothly. Line spaces between Scripture portions indicate breaks in the text.

- Ideally, with the exception of session 1, you will read the Bible Reading before your group meets so that you are prepared to jump right into the video presentation. Or, if your group meets for 90 minutes or more, volunteers may choose to take turns reading the Scripture at the beginning of the session; this will probably require at least 15 – 20 minutes. Even if you have not had opportunity to read the Bible Reading ahead of time, please attend the group anyway — the discussion questions focus on shorter passages that can be easily read on the spot.

- As you use the participant's guide and listen to Randy Frazee's video teaching, you will regularly encounter the terms *Upper Story* and *Lower Story*. What do they mean?

All through the story of the Bible two parallel and beautiful dramas unfold: There is the Upper Story. God is real, he is present, and he is working on our behalf. Heaven is breaking into the world more than we recognize, and the story of God's seeking love, perpetual grace, and longing for relationship with ordinary people is breathtaking. There is also the Lower Story. We live on earth. We make mistakes, run from God, and resist his overtures of love. Sometimes we get so mired in the Lower Story that we fail to recognize God's presence breaking into our world. We forget that the God of heaven longs to have a growing relationship, a friendship, with us. It is in *The Story of Jesus* that these two stories intertwine most significantly, as God himself entered the Lower Story through his Son and changed the course and hopes of humankind for both history and eternity.

Ultimately, God wants to be with us; with you, with me. This is the refrain that rings true through *The Story*.

Of Note

The quotes interspersed through this participant's guide are excerpts from *The Story of Jesus* video, *The Story*, and materials developed by the authors in the writing of this study.

The Birth of the King

The journey can be adventurous, and we should enjoy it. But let's be honest, there is something nice about finally arriving!

Bible Reading

In the beginning was the Word, and the Word was with God, and the Word was God. He was with God in the beginning. Through him all things were made; without him nothing was made that has been made. In him was life, and that life was the light of all mankind. The light shines in the darkness, and the darkness has not overcome it.

There was a man sent from God whose name was John. He came as a witness to testify concerning that light, so that through him all might believe. He himself was not the light; he came only as a witness to the light.

The true light that gives light to everyone was coming into the world. He was in the world, and though the world was made through him, the world did not recognize him. He came to that which was his own, but his own did not receive him. Yet to all who did receive him, to those who believed in his name, he gave the right to become children of God — children born not of natural descent, nor of human decision or a husband's will, but born of God.

The Word became flesh and made his dwelling among us. We have seen his glory, the glory of the one and only Son, who came from the Father, full of grace[1] and truth.

For the law was given through Moses; grace and truth came through Jesus Christ. No one has ever seen God, but the one and only Son, who is himself God and is in closest relationship with the Father, has made him known.

God sent the angel Gabriel to Nazareth, a town in Galilee, to a virgin pledged to be married to a man named Joseph, a descendant of David. The virgin's name was Mary. The angel went to her and said, "Greetings, you who are highly favored! The Lord is with you."

Mary was greatly troubled at his words and wondered what kind of greeting this might be. But the angel said to her, "Do not be afraid, Mary; you have found favor with God. You will conceive and give birth to a son, and you are to call him Jesus. He will be great and will be called the Son of the Most High. The Lord God will give him the throne of his father David, and he will reign over Jacob's descendants forever; his kingdom will never end."

---

[1] **Grace:** Unmerited favor and blessing. In the New Testament, this term often refers to the undeserved pardon from sin through Jesus' death.

"How will this be," Mary asked the angel, "since I am a virgin?"

The angel answered, "The Holy Spirit will come on you, and the power of the Most High will overshadow you. So the holy one to be born will be called the Son of God."

"I am the Lord's servant," Mary answered. "May your word to me be fulfilled." Then the angel left her.

And Mary said:

> "My soul glorifies the Lord
>   and my spirit rejoices in God my Savior,[2]
> for he has been mindful
>   of the humble state of his servant.
> From now on all generations will call me blessed,
>   for the Mighty One has done great things for me —
>   holy is his name.
> His mercy extends to those who fear him,
>   from generation to generation.
> He has performed mighty deeds with his arm;
>   he has scattered those who are proud in their inmost
>   thoughts.
> He has brought down rulers from their thrones
>   but has lifted up the humble.
> He has filled the hungry with good things
>   but has sent the rich away empty.
> He has helped his servant Israel,
>   remembering to be merciful
> to Abraham and his descendants forever,
>   just as he promised our ancestors."

How did Mary, a virgin, become pregnant? She and Joseph were engaged but had not had sexual relations. No medical doctor could answer this question, but such was the mysterious nature of Mary's

---

[2] **Savior:** One who rescues or heals. Jesus Christ is revealed as the Savior who rescues his people from sin and eternal punishment.

conception and Jesus' birth—a miraculous beginning ordained by God's power alone. Imagine Mary's problem explaining this incredible experience! She couldn't understand it herself, much less explain it to her friends and family.

In that day and time, an engagement was considered as strong a commitment as marriage although Joseph and Mary were not officially married. Although he probably wanted to believe Mary, Joseph was in a difficult situation. Engaged and committed to a woman whom his family and friends would now despise, Joseph decided it was best to break off the engagement . . . until an unusual visitor changed his perspective.

Because Joseph her husband was faithful to the law, and yet did not want to expose her to public disgrace, he had in mind to divorce her quietly.

But after he had considered this, an angel of the Lord appeared to him in a dream and said, "Joseph son of David, do not be afraid to take Mary home as your wife, because what is conceived in her is from the Holy Spirit. She will give birth to a son, and you are to give him the name Jesus, because he will save his people from their sins."

All this took place to fulfill what the Lord had said through the prophet: "The virgin will conceive and give birth to a son, and they will call him Immanuel" (which means "God with us").

When Joseph woke up, he did what the angel of the Lord had commanded him and took Mary home as his wife.

In those days Caesar Augustus issued a decree that a census should be taken of the entire Roman world. (This was the first census that took place while Quirinius was governor of Syria.) And everyone went to their own town to register.

So Joseph also went up from the town of Nazareth in Galilee to Judea, to Bethlehem the town of David, because he belonged to the house and line of David. He went there to register with Mary, who was pledged to be married to him and was expecting a child. While they were there, the time came for the baby to be born, and she gave birth to her firstborn, a son. She wrapped him in cloths and placed him in a manger, because there was no guest room available for them.

And there were shepherds living out in the fields nearby, keeping watch over their flocks at night. An angel of the Lord appeared to them, and the glory of the Lord shone around them, and they were terrified. But the angel said to them, "Do not be afraid. I bring you good news[3] that will cause great joy for all the people. Today in the town of David a Savior has been born to you; he is the Messiah, the Lord. This will be a sign to you: You will find a baby wrapped in cloths and lying in a manger."

Suddenly a great company of the heavenly host appeared with the angel, praising God and saying,

> "Glory to God in the highest heaven,
>   and on earth peace to those on whom his favor rests."

When the angels had left them and gone into heaven, the shepherds said to one another, "Let's go to Bethlehem and see this thing that has happened, which the Lord has told us about."

So they hurried off and found Mary and Joseph, and the baby, who was lying in the manger. When they had seen him, they spread the word concerning what had been told them about this child, and all who heard it were amazed at what the shepherds said to them. But Mary treasured up all these things and pondered them in her heart. The shepherds returned, glorifying and praising God for all the things they had heard and seen, which were just as they had been told.

Joseph and Mary decided to remain in Bethlehem after Jesus was born. Faithful to the Law of Moses, they had Jesus circumcised when he was eight days old. There the new family was greeted by two older saints, Simeon and Anna, to whom God gave the opportunity to see and recognize the Messiah before the end of their days. And these wouldn't be the last individuals to discern the special nature of the child Jesus.

After Jesus was born in Bethlehem in Judea, during the time of King Herod, Magi[4] from the east came to Jerusalem and asked, "Where is the one who has been born king of the Jews? We saw his star when it rose

---

[3] **Good news:** The literal translation of the word *gospel*, this word refers to the message that Jesus has come to reconcile humanity to God. The good news is that each individual can accept this undeserved gift and enter into a relationship with him.

[4] **Magi:** Traditionally *wise men*.

and have come to worship him."

When King Herod heard this he was disturbed, and all Jerusalem with him. When he had called together all the people's chief priests and teachers of the law, he asked them where the Messiah was to be born. "In Bethlehem in Judea," they replied, "for this is what the prophet has written:

"'But you, Bethlehem, in the land of Judah,
    are by no means least among the rulers of Judah;
for out of you will come a ruler
    who will shepherd my people Israel.'"

Then Herod called the Magi secretly and found out from them the exact time the star had appeared. He sent them to Bethlehem and said, "Go and search carefully for the child. As soon as you find him, report to me, so that I too may go and worship him."

After they had heard the king, they went on their way, and the star they had seen when it rose went ahead of them until it stopped over the place where the child was. When they saw the star, they were overjoyed. On coming to the house, they saw the child with his mother Mary, and they bowed down and worshiped him. Then they opened their treasures and presented him with gifts of gold, frankincense and myrrh. And having been warned in a dream not to go back to Herod, they returned to their country by another route.

When they had gone, an angel of the Lord appeared to Joseph in a dream. "Get up," he said, "take the child and his mother and escape to Egypt. Stay there until I tell you, for Herod is going to search for the child to kill him."

So he got up, took the child and his mother during the night and left for Egypt, where he stayed until the death of Herod. And so was fulfilled what the Lord had said through the prophet: "Out of Egypt I called my son."

When Herod realized that he had been outwitted by the Magi, he was furious, and he gave orders to kill all the boys in Bethlehem and its vicinity who were two years old and under, in accordance with the time he had learned from the Magi. Then what was said through the prophet Jeremiah was fulfilled:

"A voice is heard in Ramah,
    weeping and great mourning,

Rachel weeping for her children
and refusing to be comforted,
because they are no more."

After Herod died, an angel of the Lord appeared in a dream to Joseph in Egypt and said, "Get up, take the child and his mother and go to the land of Israel, for those who were trying to take the child's life are dead."

So he got up, took the child and his mother and went to the land of Israel. But when he heard that Archelaus was reigning in Judea in place of his father Herod, he was afraid to go there. Having been warned in a dream, he withdrew to the district of Galilee, and he went and lived in a town called Nazareth.

Nothing more is known about the boy Jesus until he appears in Jerusalem at age 12. Most likely he learned carpentry skills as a youngster from Joseph and studied in the synagogue. His mind grew strong, along with his body and soul. While still a youth, his agile mind was ready to engage in discussion with synagogue leaders. One time Jesus became so engrossed in learning and questioning that he lost track of time.

Every year Jesus' parents went to Jerusalem for the Festival of the Passover. When he was twelve years old, they went up to the festival, according to the custom. After the festival was over, while his parents were returning home, the boy Jesus stayed behind in Jerusalem, but they were unaware of it. Thinking he was in their company, they traveled on for a day. Then they began looking for him among their relatives and friends. When they did not find him, they went back to Jerusalem to look for him. After three days they found him in the temple courts, sitting among the teachers, listening to them and asking them questions. Everyone who heard him was amazed at his understanding and his answers. When his parents saw him, they were astonished. His mother said to him, "Son, why have you treated us like this? Your father and I have been anxiously searching for you."

"Why were you searching for me?" he asked. "Didn't you know I had to be in my Father's house?" But they did not understand what he was saying to them.

Then he went down to Nazareth with them and was obedient to them.

But his mother treasured all these things in her heart. And Jesus grew in wisdom and stature, and in favor with God and man.

Who was this Jesus? A new prophet? A scholar destined to be a great rabbi? Perhaps a political leader with the charisma to finally send the oppressive Roman armies, who controlled Judea, back across the sea? None of these expectations turned out to describe him adequately. In fact, Jesus defied expectations as the people watched and wondered.

— Includes portions of Matthew 1 – 2; Luke 1 – 2; and John 1

Participant's Guide

Introduction

From all over the United States and beyond, people visit the Grand Canyon in Arizona so they can feast their eyes on one of the most amazing natural wonders on the face of this planet.

The thing about the Grand Canyon is that snapshots and videos simply don't do justice to its grandeur. Friends can try to describe it and artists can paint pictures, but nothing compares with breathing in the beauty and breathtaking majesty of it all.

If you have made this pilgrimage you might have vivid memories of kids in the backseat asking, for the hundredth time, "Are we there yet?" Then, finally, as the moment arrives, all the hours of travel seem like nothing as you stand on the edge of the sheer drop-off and your eyes span the chasm. An almost holy hush falls over those you have traveled with ... you stand in awe!

Every page of *The Story* up to now (the entire account of humankind, specifically of God's people Israel recorded in the Old Testament) we have been on the journey, wondering when we will get there. Today we have arrived. We look into the manger and behold the Lord of Glory, "God with us," the long-awaited Messiah.

Let a holy hush fall over your heart. Look closely. This is the one who made the Grand Canyon, the heavens and the earth ... and everything in them. God in a manger. We have arrived!

Talk About It

Tell about a time you traveled a long way to see someone or something and describe how it felt when you finally arrived.

Video Teaching Notes

As you watch the video segment for session 1, use the following outline to record anything that stands out to you.

I. Lower Story: scandalous beginnings

II. Upper Story: God's solution to our scandalous beginnings

III. God comes down to bring us back to himself

IV. The fulfillment of many prophecies

Video Discussion

1. *The Story* began in Genesis 1 – 3, and the Jews in Jesus' day had read and heard it over and over throughout their lives. What would have come to their minds when the story of Jesus (the solution to all our problems) began with the same words that started *The Story*, back before there was any sin in the world?

2. Various titles and descriptions of Jesus are included in his story (John 1:1 – 14; included in the session's Bible Reading). Pick one of the following and explain what you think it means and how you have experienced this to be true of Jesus:

   Jesus: The Word

   Jesus: Is God

   Jesus: The Maker of all things

   Jesus: The Life

   Jesus: The Light

   Jesus: The one and only Son

   Jesus: The one who brings grace and truth

3. God spoke to both Mary and Joseph through angels (Luke 1:26 – 38; Matthew 1:19 – 24; included in the session's Bible Reading). What was the angel's message and how did Mary and Joseph respond to this heavenly messenger?

> *Jesus' birth is not the result of a scandal ...*
> *but a solution to our scandal—our sin.*

4. Pause to remember that Mary and Joseph were real people living in a real small town. How might Joseph's family and the townspeople have responded when Mary turned up pregnant before the wedding day? How might they have reacted to the "An angel told me that God would make me pregnant, but Joseph and I are still virgins" story?

Tell about a time that God called you to live for him or follow him in a way that others did not understand. How did you hold to your faith during this time?

5. Jesus was born of a virgin and was conceived without sin. Why does this matter?

> *From the Lower Story it looked like this baby would be born in sin, but from the Upper Story we see that Jesus was born without sin.*

6. In the Lower Story Joseph and Mary had to go to Bethlehem to be counted in the census; it was a hard three-day journey for someone nine months pregnant. In the Upper Story God was getting them to Bethlehem because that is where the Messiah was to be born. Recall an event in your life that seemed inconvenient and unnecessary, only to later look back and realize God was doing something greater than you knew at the time.

7. After Jesus was born, the shepherds hurried off and told everyone what they had seen and heard. Share a brief testimony about a time you really saw or heard Jesus move in your life. How might you share this story (and others like it) outside your small group ... with people who are not yet followers of Jesus?

8. Jesus is Immanuel, "God with us" (Matthew 1:23; included in the session's Bible Reading). As you walk with Jesus your Savior, how does it help you to know that he is God and that he is with you ... all the time?

In what situation do you need to be reminded that God is with you? How can your small group members pray for you as you walk through this season of your life?

Closing Prayer

As you take time to pray, here are some ideas to get you started:

- Thank God that his Upper Story work is always the right thing, even when we don't fully understand what he is doing.
- Pray for courage to follow God, even when it is hard.
- Pray for eyes to see Jesus as he is: the Light, the Life, Immanuel, the Son of God, God, the Savior, and so much more!

Between Sessions

Personal Reflections

If we could really get hold of the truth of being freed from our sins, we would be filled with unspeakable joy. Thank God for sending his Son to pay the price of your sins. Praise Jesus for the great love he demonstrated by sacrificing himself on the cross.

Personal Action

At the end of the video segment, Randy talked about how Jesus wants to do three distinct things in and through us. In the coming week pray about and then identify one action you can take to grow in each of these three areas:

- Jesus wants to come in you. (Invite him to dwell fully in you by his Spirit.)
- He wants to grow in you. (Pray that you will go deeper and deeper in faith.)
- He wants to come out of you. (Ask Jesus to let his light shine through you and touch the lives of others.)

Read for Next Session

Take time before your next small group to read the Bible Reading for session 2, "Jesus' Ministry Begins." And, if you have the opportunity, also go back and read the session 1 Bible Reading.

Jesus'
Ministry Begins

God's solution for our sin problem is not a "What" but a "Who."

Bible Reading

Imagine if you were introducing the Savior of the world. Wouldn't you make it a gala event? Call in the media? Spotlight the attending celebs? Give the Savior the red-carpet treatment? Get people's attention?

God doesn't work that way. He planned his Son's introduction using a scruffy bohemian prophet called John the Baptist. John, the son of Mary's relative Elizabeth, was the one who had been foretold to precede the Messiah "in the spirit and power of Elijah." John was unique among the prophets. He lived outside of the mainstream religious culture, yet his message was more timely than any other.

In those days John the Baptist came, preaching in the wilderness of Judea and saying, "Repent, for the kingdom of heaven has come near."

John's clothes were made of camel's hair, and he had a leather belt around his waist. His food was locusts and wild honey. People went out to him from Jerusalem and all Judea and the whole region of the Jordan. Confessing their sins, they were baptized[1] by him in the Jordan River.

Then Jesus came from Galilee to the Jordan to be baptized by John. But John tried to deter him, saying, "I need to be baptized by you, and do you come to me?"

Jesus replied, "Let it be so now; it is proper for us to do this to fulfill all righteousness." Then John consented.

As soon as Jesus was baptized, he went up out of the water. At that moment heaven was opened, and he saw the Spirit of God descending like a dove and alighting on him. And a voice from heaven said, "This is my Son, whom I love; with him I am well pleased."

Then Jesus was led by the Spirit into the wilderness to be tempted by the devil. After fasting forty days and forty nights, he was hungry. The tempter came to him and said, "If you are the Son of God, tell these stones to become bread."

Jesus answered, "It is written: 'Man shall not live on bread alone, but on every word that comes from the mouth of God.' "

Then the devil took him to the holy city and had him stand on the

---

[1] **Baptized, baptism:** A symbolic act demonstrating that new believers have abandoned their former ways and have embarked on new life.

highest point of the temple. "If you are the Son of God," he said, "throw yourself down. For it is written:

> "'He will command his angels concerning you,
>> and they will lift you up in their hands,
>> so that you will not strike your foot against a stone.'"

Jesus answered him, "It is also written: 'Do not put the Lord your God to the test.'"

Again, the devil took him to a very high mountain and showed him all the kingdoms of the world and their splendor. "All this I will give you," he said, "if you will bow down and worship me."

Jesus said to him, "Away from me, Satan! For it is written: 'Worship the Lord your God, and serve him only.'"

Then the devil left him, and angels came and attended him.

Following the test in the wilderness, Jesus began his public ministry. John the Baptist continued to point to Jesus, claiming that everything God had promised centered on this one man. This was startling news to the religious elite, and John was asked to explain himself. Imagine skilled religious lawyers questioning this rough-hewn eccentric, a man without credentials or authorization. The interrogation began.

Now this was John's testimony when the Jewish leaders in Jerusalem sent priests and Levites to ask him who he was. He did not fail to confess, but confessed freely, "I am not the Messiah."

They asked him, "Then who are you? Are you Elijah?"

He said, "I am not."

"Are you the Prophet?"

He answered, "No."

Finally they said, "Who are you? Give us an answer to take back to those who sent us. What do you say about yourself?"

John replied in the words of Isaiah the prophet, "I am the voice of one calling in the wilderness, 'Make straight the way for the Lord.'"

Now the Pharisees[2] who had been sent questioned him, "Why then do

---

[2] **Pharisees:** The most powerful group of religious authorities within Judaism. The Pharisees were highly focused on their interpretation of the laws given by God, and they often challenged Jesus regarding these precepts.

you baptize if you are not the Messiah, nor Elijah, nor the Prophet?"

"I baptize with water," John replied, "but among you stands one you do not know. He is the one who comes after me, the straps of whose sandals I am not worthy to untie."

This all happened at Bethany on the other side of the Jordan, where John was baptizing.

The next day John saw Jesus coming toward him and said, "Look, the Lamb of God,[3] who takes away the sin of the world! This is the one I meant when I said, 'A man who comes after me has surpassed me because he was before me.' I myself did not know him, but the reason I came baptizing with water was that he might be revealed to Israel."

Then John gave this testimony: "I saw the Spirit come down from heaven as a dove and remain on him. And I myself did not know him, but the one who sent me to baptize with water told me, 'The man on whom you see the Spirit come down and remain is the one who will baptize with the Holy Spirit.' I have seen and I testify that this is God's Chosen One."

The next day John was there again with two of his disciples.[4] When he saw Jesus passing by, he said, "Look, the Lamb of God!"

When the two disciples heard him say this, they followed Jesus. Turning around, Jesus saw them following and asked, "What do you want?"

They said, "Rabbi" (which means "Teacher"), "where are you staying?"

"Come," he replied, "and you will see."

So they went and saw where he was staying, and they spent that day with him. It was about four in the afternoon.

Andrew, Simon Peter's brother, was one of the two who heard what John had said and who had followed Jesus. The first thing Andrew did was to find his brother Simon and tell him, "We have found the Messiah" (that is, the Christ). And he brought him to Jesus.

Jesus looked at him and said, "You are Simon son of John. You will be called Cephas" (which, when translated, is Peter).[5]

The next day Jesus decided to leave for Galilee. Finding Philip, he said to him, "Follow me."

Philip, like Andrew and Peter, was from the town of Bethsaida. Philip found Nathanael and told him, "We have found the one Moses wrote

---

[3] **Lamb of God:** One of the names of Jesus, which demonstrates the connection between Jesus' sacrificial death and the offerings of the Old Testament.

[4] **Disciples:** The followers of Jesus.

[5] **Peter:** *Cephas* (Aramaic) and *Peter* (Greek) both mean "rock."

about in the Law, and about whom the prophets also wrote—Jesus of Nazareth, the son of Joseph."

"Nazareth! Can anything good come from there?" Nathanael asked.

"Come and see," said Philip.

When Jesus saw Nathanael approaching, he said of him, "Here truly is an Israelite in whom there is no deceit."

"How do you know me?" Nathanael asked.

Jesus answered, "I saw you while you were still under the fig tree before Philip called you."

Then Nathanael declared, "Rabbi, you are the Son of God; you are the king of Israel."

Jesus said, "You believe because I told you I saw you under the fig tree. You will see greater things than that." He then added, "Very truly I tell you, you will see 'heaven open, and the angels of God ascending and descending on' the Son of Man."[6]

On the third day a wedding took place at Cana in Galilee. Jesus' mother was there, and Jesus and his disciples had also been invited to the wedding. When the wine was gone, Jesus' mother said to him, "They have no more wine."

"Woman, why do you involve me?" Jesus replied. "My hour has not yet come."

His mother said to the servants, "Do whatever he tells you."

Nearby stood six stone water jars, the kind used by the Jews for ceremonial washing, each holding from twenty to thirty gallons.

Jesus said to the servants, "Fill the jars with water"; so they filled them to the brim.

Then he told them, "Now draw some out and take it to the master of the banquet."

They did so, and the master of the banquet tasted the water that had been turned into wine. He did not realize where it had come from, though the servants who had drawn the water knew. Then he called the bridegroom aside and said, "Everyone brings out the choice wine first and then the cheaper wine after the guests have had too much to drink; but you have saved the best till now."

What Jesus did here in Cana of Galilee was the first of the signs through which he revealed his glory; and his disciples believed in him.

---

[6] **Son of Man:** A name of Jesus that emphasizes his dual nature as both fully God and fully human.

Jesus began to reveal who he was, and he was like no other person anyone had known. Although he was fully human, he was also fully God. With his 12 disciples as interns, Jesus began his itinerant ministry of teaching and healing.

Soon he traveled to the city of Jerusalem to celebrate the Passover feast. It was in Jerusalem that political and religious decisions were made; power brokers set their agendas in this bustling town. Many people listened to Jesus' teachings and believed he was the Messiah. Others thought he was a troublemaker. One inquisitive religious leader sought Jesus out privately, under cover of darkness. Jesus took the opportunity to summarize his mission by talking about being born … again.

Now there was a Pharisee, a man named Nicodemus who was a member of the Jewish ruling council. He came to Jesus at night and said, "Rabbi, we know that you are a teacher who has come from God. For no one could perform the signs you are doing if God were not with him."

Jesus replied, "Very truly I tell you, no one can see the kingdom of God unless they are born again."[7]

"How can someone be born when they are old?" Nicodemus asked. "Surely they cannot enter a second time into their mother's womb to be born!"

Jesus answered, "Very truly I tell you, no one can enter the kingdom of God unless they are born of water and the Spirit. Flesh gives birth to flesh, but the Spirit gives birth to spirit. You should not be surprised at my saying, 'You must be born again.' The wind blows wherever it pleases. You hear its sound, but you cannot tell where it comes from or where it is going. So it is with everyone born of the Spirit."

"How can this be?" Nicodemus asked.

"You are Israel's teacher," said Jesus, "and do you not understand these things? Very truly I tell you, we speak of what we know, and we testify to what we have seen, but still you people do not accept our testimony. I have spoken to you of earthly things and you do not believe; how then will you believe if I speak of heavenly things? No one has ever gone into heaven except the one who came from heaven — the Son of

---

[7] **Born again:** A term signifying the new spiritual life gained when one believes in Jesus Christ as the Son of God and accepts his death on the cross as a "free gift" that releases people from the penalty of sin.

Man. Just as Moses lifted up the snake in the wilderness, so the Son of Man must be lifted up, that everyone who believes may have eternal life in him."

For God so loved the world that he gave his one and only Son, that whoever believes in him shall not perish but have eternal life. For God did not send his Son into the world to condemn the world, but to save the world through him. Whoever believes in him is not condemned, but whoever does not believe stands condemned already because they have not believed in the name of God's one and only Son.

The kind of claims Jesus made did not make him very popular with the religious elite. But Jesus knew his purpose, and he spent much of his time with ordinary people who had ordinary human needs. One such person was a woman he met in the region of Samaria. Women were second-class citizens in the culture of that day. In addition, there was a harsh rivalry between Jews and Samaritans, and most Jews would not associate in any way with Samaritans, let alone a woman. But once again, Jesus broke the mold.

Now he had to go through Samaria. So he came to a town in Samaria called Sychar, near the plot of ground Jacob had given to his son Joseph. Jacob's well was there, and Jesus, tired as he was from the journey, sat down by the well. It was about noon.

When a Samaritan woman came to draw water, Jesus said to her, "Will you give me a drink?" (His disciples had gone into the town to buy food.)

The Samaritan woman said to him, "You are a Jew and I am a Samaritan woman. How can you ask me for a drink?" (For Jews do not associate with Samaritans.)

Jesus answered her, "If you knew the gift of God and who it is that asks you for a drink, you would have asked him and he would have given you living water."

"Sir," the woman said, "you have nothing to draw with and the well is deep. Where can you get this living water? Are you greater than our father Jacob, who gave us the well and drank from it himself, as did also his sons and his livestock?"

Jesus answered, "Everyone who drinks this water will be thirsty again, but whoever drinks the water I give them will never thirst. Indeed, the water I give them will become in them a spring of water welling up to eternal life."

The woman said to him, "Sir, give me this water so that I won't get thirsty and have to keep coming here to draw water."

He told her, "Go, call your husband and come back."

"I have no husband," she replied.

Jesus said to her, "You are right when you say you have no husband. The fact is, you have had five husbands, and the man you now have is not your husband. What you have just said is quite true."

"Sir," the woman said, "I can see that you are a prophet. Our ancestors worshiped on this mountain, but you Jews claim that the place where we must worship is in Jerusalem."

"Woman," Jesus replied, "believe me, a time is coming when you will worship the Father neither on this mountain nor in Jerusalem. You Samaritans worship what you do not know; we worship what we do know, for salvation is from the Jews. Yet a time is coming and has now come when the true worshipers will worship the Father in the Spirit and in truth, for they are the kind of worshipers the Father seeks. God is spirit, and his worshipers must worship in the Spirit and in truth."

The woman said, "I know that Messiah" (called Christ) "is coming. When he comes, he will explain everything to us."

Then Jesus declared, "I, the one speaking to you — I am he."

Just then his disciples returned and were surprised to find him talking with a woman. But no one asked, "What do you want?" or "Why are you talking with her?"

Then, leaving her water jar, the woman went back to the town and said to the people, "Come, see a man who told me everything I ever did. Could this be the Messiah?" They came out of the town and made their way toward him.

Many of the Samaritans from that town believed in him because of the woman's testimony, "He told me everything I ever did." So when the Samaritans came to him, they urged him to stay with them, and he stayed two days. And because of his words many more became believers.

They said to the woman, "We no longer believe just because of what you said; now we have heard for ourselves, and we know that this man really is the Savior of the world."

After the two days he left for Galilee.

They went to Capernaum, and when the Sabbath came, Jesus went into the synagogue and began to teach. The people were amazed at his teaching, because he taught them as one who had authority, not as the teachers of the law. Just then a man in their synagogue who was possessed by an impure spirit cried out, "What do you want with us, Jesus of Nazareth? Have you come to destroy us? I know who you are — the Holy One of God!"

"Be quiet!" said Jesus sternly. "Come out of him!" The impure spirit shook the man violently and came out of him with a shriek.

The people were all so amazed that they asked each other, "What is this? A new teaching — and with authority! He even gives orders to impure spirits and they obey him." News about him spread quickly over the whole region of Galilee.

As soon as they left the synagogue, they went with James and John to the home of Simon and Andrew. Simon's mother-in-law was in bed with a fever, and they immediately told Jesus about her. So he went to her, took her hand and helped her up. The fever left her and she began to wait on them.

That evening after sunset the people brought to Jesus all the sick and demon-possessed. The whole town gathered at the door, and Jesus healed many who had various diseases. He also drove out many demons, but he would not let the demons speak because they knew who he was.

Very early in the morning, while it was still dark, Jesus got up, left the house and went off to a solitary place, where he prayed. Simon and his companions went to look for him, and when they found him, they exclaimed: "Everyone is looking for you!"

Jesus replied, "Let us go somewhere else — to the nearby villages — so I can preach there also. That is why I have come." So he traveled throughout Galilee, preaching in their synagogues and driving out demons.

A man with leprosy came to him and begged him on his knees, "If you are willing, you can make me clean."

Jesus was indignant. He reached out his hand and touched the man. "I am willing," he said. "Be clean!" Immediately the leprosy left him and he was cleansed.

Jesus sent him away at once with a strong warning: "See that you don't tell this to anyone. But go, show yourself to the priest and offer the sacrifices that Moses commanded for your cleansing, as a testimony to them."

Instead he went out and began to talk freely, spreading the news. As a result, Jesus could no longer enter a town openly but stayed outside in lonely places. Yet the people still came to him from everywhere.

A few days later, when Jesus again entered Capernaum, the people heard that he had come home. They gathered in such large numbers that there was no room left, not even outside the door, and he preached the word to them. Some men came, bringing to him a paralyzed man, carried by four of them. Since they could not get him to Jesus because of the crowd, they made an opening in the roof above Jesus by digging through it and then lowered the mat the man was lying on. When Jesus saw their faith, he said to the paralyzed man, "Son, your sins are forgiven."

Now some teachers of the law were sitting there, thinking to themselves, "Why does this fellow talk like that? He's blaspheming! Who can forgive sins but God alone?"

Immediately Jesus knew in his spirit that this was what they were thinking in their hearts, and he said to them, "Why are you thinking these things? Which is easier: to say to this paralyzed man, 'Your sins are forgiven,' or to say, 'Get up, take your mat and walk'? But I want you to know that the Son of Man has authority on earth to forgive sins." So he said to the man, "I tell you, get up, take your mat and go home." He got up, took his mat and walked out in full view of them all. This amazed everyone and they praised God, saying, "We have never seen anything like this!"

Once again Jesus went out beside the lake. A large crowd came to him, and he began to teach them. As he walked along, he saw Levi son of Alphaeus sitting at the tax collector's booth. "Follow me," Jesus told him, and Levi got up and followed him.

While Jesus was having dinner at Levi's house, many tax collectors and sinners were eating with him and his disciples, for there were many who followed him. When the teachers of the law who were Pharisees saw him eating with the sinners and tax collectors, they asked his disciples: "Why does he eat with tax collectors and sinners?"

On hearing this, Jesus said to them, "It is not the healthy who need a doctor, but the sick. I have not come to call the righteous, but sinners."

From the start, Jesus appeared to be a different kind of rabbi. He seemed to disregard the many customary laws that defined proper behavior for Jewish people. He put people before laws. His "new way" was forgiving and kind. Jesus didn't come off as a rabble-

rouser but as a friend to people on the outside, people suspected of not being pure, people most religious leaders disliked.

Another time Jesus went into the synagogue, and a man with a shriveled hand was there. Some of them were looking for a reason to accuse Jesus, so they watched him closely to see if he would heal him on the Sabbath. Jesus said to the man with the shriveled hand, "Stand up in front of everyone."

Then Jesus asked them, "Which is lawful on the Sabbath: to do good or to do evil, to save life or to kill?" But they remained silent.

He looked around at them in anger and, deeply distressed at their stubborn hearts, said to the man, "Stretch out your hand." He stretched it out, and his hand was completely restored. Then the Pharisees went out and began to plot with the Herodians[8] how they might kill Jesus.

Jesus went throughout Galilee, teaching in their synagogues, proclaiming the good news of the kingdom, and healing every disease and sickness among the people. News about him spread all over Syria, and people brought to him all who were ill with various diseases, those suffering severe pain, the demon-possessed, those having seizures, and the paralyzed; and he healed them. Large crowds from Galilee, the Decapolis, Jerusalem, Judea and the region across the Jordan followed him.

Because of the crowd he told his disciples to have a small boat ready for him, to keep the people from crowding him. For he had healed many, so that those with diseases were pushing forward to touch him. Whenever the impure spirits saw him, they fell down before him and cried out, "You are the Son of God." But he gave them strict orders not to tell others about him.

The Jews were convinced that when the long-awaited Messiah came, he would free the people from political oppression. He would liberate them from the power of the Roman Empire. They were looking for an earthly king to bring their nation into power. But Jesus' purpose was much deeper, his intentions more significant, and his kingship infinitely more glorious than what the people were expecting. They had to learn the true meaning of the word

---

[8] **Herodians:** A Jewish sect.

"Messiah"—Anointed One. They had to discover who Jesus really was. Only then would they have his okay to spread the Good News.

Jesus went up on a mountainside and called to him those he wanted, and they came to him. He appointed twelve that they might be with him and that he might send them out to preach and to have authority to drive out demons. These are the twelve he appointed: Simon (to whom he gave the name Peter), James son of Zebedee and his brother John (to them he gave the name Boanerges, which means "sons of thunder"), Andrew, Philip, Bartholomew, Matthew, Thomas, James son of Alphaeus, Thaddaeus, Simon the Zealot and Judas Iscariot, who betrayed him.

After this, Jesus traveled about from one town and village to another, proclaiming the good news of the kingdom of God. The Twelve were with him, and also some women who had been cured of evil spirits and diseases: Mary (called Magdalene) from whom seven demons had come out; Joanna the wife of Chuza, the manager of Herod's household; Susanna; and many others. These women were helping to support them out of their own means.

Apparently even John the Baptist didn't really understand who Jesus was. John had announced Jesus as the coming Messiah, but Jesus' work hadn't brought the results John evidently expected. Added to John's disappointment was the fact that he had been languishing in prison for some time because he had publicly criticized Herod Antipas.

Herod Antipas was one of the sons of Herod the Great, who ruled at the time of Jesus' birth. Herod Antipas was the Roman puppet ruler over Galilee, and he had convinced his brother's wife to leave her husband and marry him, a violation of Jewish law. John had been locked up for pointing out Herod's sin.

When John, who was in prison, heard about the deeds of the Messiah, he sent his disciples to ask him, "Are you the one who is to come, or should we expect someone else?"

Jesus replied, "Go back and report to John what you hear and see: The blind receive sight, the lame walk, those who have leprosy are cleansed, the deaf hear, the dead are raised, and the good news is proclaimed to the poor. Blessed is anyone who does not stumble on account of me."

As John's disciples were leaving, Jesus began to speak to the crowd about John: "What did you go out into the wilderness to see? A reed swayed by the wind? If not, what did you go out to see? A man dressed in fine clothes? No, those who wear fine clothes are in kings' palaces. Then what did you go out to see? A prophet? Yes, I tell you, and more than a prophet. This is the one about whom it is written:

> "'I will send my messenger ahead of you,
>   who will prepare your way before you.'

Truly I tell you, among those born of women there has not risen anyone greater than John the Baptist; yet whoever is least in the kingdom of heaven is greater than he. From the days of John the Baptist until now, the kingdom of heaven has been subjected to violence, and violent people have been raiding it. For all the Prophets and the Law prophesied until John. And if you are willing to accept it, he is the Elijah who was to come."

Jesus' answer to John gave more insight into Jesus' role as Savior and the Messiah. Many people were intrigued by this prophet and teacher, and they wanted to hear more.

— Includes portions of Matthew 3 – 4, 11; Mark 1 – 3; Luke 8; and John 1 – 4

Participant's Guide

Introduction

Religion is always about "What." What am I supposed to do? What should I stop doing? What clothes should I wear? What words can't I say anymore? What will people think of me? And the hit parade of "Whats" just keeps going!

By this point in *The Story* the people of Israel had compiled a massive list of "Whats" in an attempt to please God and show that they were worthy of his love and acceptance. Some religious leaders of that day had become experts in telling everyone else what they were supposed to do.

Into this climate God breaks in with his Upper Story and surprises everyone. Salvation is not based on a list of what we do to make God happy and what we won't do because it is against the rules. Of course, God cares about our behavior and wants his children to grow in holiness, but this is not his first concern. Before we begin thinking about being good people, we need to meet the One who can help us become good.

The solution to the problem, way back in the first century, was not a "What" but a "Who." It was all about Jesus. Now, two thousand years later, it is exactly the same. Before we begin thinking about the "What," we need to meet the "Who." He is still Jesus!

Talk About It

Some people today still think salvation is about a list of do's and don'ts. When people head down this road, what are some things they put on the "What we have to do" list and the "What we can't do" list?

Video Teaching Notes

As you watch the video segment for session 2, use the following outline to record anything that stands out to you.

I. John the Baptist introduces us to God's solution

II. Jesus is the Lamb of God

III. Encounters that teach us Jesus is the "Who" we have been waiting for

IV. John the Baptist dies knowing who Jesus is

Video Discussion

1. At the baptism of Jesus (Matthew 3:13 – 17; included in the session's Bible Reading), what did the people see and hear, and how did this clarify who Jesus was?

> John the Baptist tells us that the solution to our problem is not a "What" but a "Who." We have to understand who he is before we can understand what he came to do. What he is going to do will only make a difference if he is who he says he is.

2. After forty days in the wilderness Jesus faced three temptations from the devil (Matthew 4:1 – 11; included in the session's Bible Reading). What was each temptation and what did Jesus say to fend off each? How does Satan use similar types of temptation in our lives today?

3. How can knowing Scripture help us battle against daily temptations? Tell about a time you used Scripture to stand strong against the enemy.

4. An earlier episode of *The Story* told of the Passover lamb (Exodus 12:1 – 30) which was slain and whose blood was placed on the doorpost to protect God's people in Egypt from the angel of death. Now John the Baptist calls Jesus "the Lamb of God, who takes away the sins of the world" (John 1:29; included in the session's Bible Reading). First-century Jews knew all about the Passover and the sacrificial system. What message would John's words about Jesus have sent them and what message should it send us today?

> *Jesus is the Lamb of God. No Jewish person could have misunderstood what John was saying. The young, unblemished, innocent lamb of the Old Testament was the one whose life was given up and whose blood was shed to pay for sins.*

5. As Jesus called people to follow him, many immediately invited someone else to meet the Savior. Who has God placed in your life that you
   would like to invite to know Jesus? How can your group members pray
   for you as you seek to reach out to this person with God's love and grace?

6. In Jesus' encounter with Nicodemus (John 3:1 – 21; included in the session's Bible Reading), Jesus talked about the Upper Story while Nicodemus focused on the Lower Story. How do you see these two stories
   conflicting in their conversation? How did Jesus help Nicodemus think
   in Upper Story terms?

   What does Jesus reveal to Nicodemus and to us about the heart of God,
   heaven, and judgment in this passage?

7. Jesus told the woman at the well that God looks for people who will
   worship the Father in Spirit and in truth (John 4:21 – 24; included in the
   session's Bible Reading). What helps you connect with God's Holy Spirit?
   What helps you grow more authentic and truthful as you worship?

8. Jesus sought out quiet places where he could meet with the Father face-to-face (Mark 1:35; included in the session's Bible Reading). Why is it important that Christians today make regular time to be quiet before God? How are you doing in this area and how can your group members support you in this discipline of spiritual growth?

Closing Prayer

As you take time to pray, here are some ideas to get you started:

- Pray that we will recognize Jesus in our midst, throughout each day of our lives.
- Ask God to help you notice when his Upper Story is breaking into your life.
- Praise Jesus for coming as our Messiah and the Savior of the world.

Between Sessions

Personal Reflections

It really is all about the "Who." Spend time reflecting on who Jesus is, letting the stories in this chapter of *The Story* guide you. What do you learn about Jesus as you:

- Watch him being baptized
- Listen to John the Baptist talk about him
- See him calling followers
- Listen to his conversation with Nicodemus
- Hear the woman at the well talk with him
- See him heal the sick and cast out demons
- Consider how he dealt with the religious leaders of his day

Personal Action

When Jesus called Levi (Matthew) to follow him, new relational bridges were built (Mark 2:13 – 17; included in the session's Bible Reading). Matthew invited Jesus to his house for a party and also invited all his "old friends," who happened to be tax collectors, prostitutes, and sinners.

When Christians invite committed believers and nonbelievers to a place where they can connect relationally, good things can happen. Consider planning a party or dinner and invite both committed Christians and spiritual seekers. Pray for God to do great things ... and see what he does.

Read for Next Session

Take time before your next small group to read the Bible Reading for session 3, "No Ordinary Man."

No Ordinary Man

Some people might call reading, writing, and arithmetic the fundamentals, but when Jesus entered the classroom of history, he taught what matters most of all.

Bible Reading

Again Jesus began to teach by the lake. The crowd that gathered around him was so large that he got into a boat and sat in it out on the lake, while all the people were along the shore at the water's edge. He taught them many things by parables, and in his teaching said: "Listen! A farmer went out to sow his seed. As he was scattering the seed, some fell along the path, and the birds came and ate it up. Some fell on rocky places, where it did not have much soil. It sprang up quickly, because the soil was shallow. But when the sun came up, the plants were scorched, and they withered because they had no root. Other seed fell among thorns, which grew up and choked the plants, so that they did not bear grain. Still other seed fell on good soil. It came up, grew and produced a crop, some multiplying thirty, some sixty, some a hundred times."

Then Jesus said, "Whoever has ears to hear, let them hear."

When he was alone, the Twelve and the others around him asked him about the parables. He told them, "The secret of the kingdom of God has been given to you. But to those on the outside everything is said in parables so that,

> "'they may be ever seeing but never perceiving,
> and ever hearing but never understanding;
> otherwise they might turn and be forgiven!'"

Then Jesus said to them, "Don't you understand this parable? How then will you understand any parable? The farmer sows the word. Some people are like seed along the path, where the word is sown. As soon as they hear it, Satan comes and takes away the word that was sown in them. Others, like seed sown on rocky places, hear the word and at once receive it with joy. But since they have no root, they last only a short time. When trouble or persecution comes because of the word, they quickly fall away. Still others, like seed sown among thorns, hear the word; but the worries of this life, the deceitfulness of wealth and the desires for other things come in and choke the word, making it unfruitful. Others, like seed sown on good soil, hear the word, accept it, and produce a crop — some thirty, some sixty, some a hundred times what was sown."

He said to them, "Do you bring in a lamp to put it under a bowl or a bed? Instead, don't you put it on its stand? For whatever is hidden is meant to be disclosed, and whatever is concealed is meant to be brought out into the open. If anyone has ears to hear, let them hear.

"Consider carefully what you hear," he continued. "With the measure you use, it will be measured to you — and even more. Whoever has will be given more; whoever does not have, even what they have will be taken from them."

He also said, "This is what the kingdom of God is like. A man scatters seed on the ground. Night and day, whether he sleeps or gets up, the seed sprouts and grows, though he does not know how. All by itself the soil produces grain — first the stalk, then the head, then the full kernel in the head. As soon as the grain is ripe, he puts the sickle to it, because the harvest has come."

Again he said, "What shall we say the kingdom of God is like, or what parable shall we use to describe it? It is like a mustard seed, which is the smallest of all seeds on earth. Yet when planted, it grows and becomes the largest of all garden plants, with such big branches that the birds can perch in its shade."

With many similar parables Jesus spoke the word to them, as much as they could understand. He did not say anything to them without using a parable. But when he was alone with his own disciples, he explained everything.

Jesus often used parables to teach the people. These stories, typically drawn from nature or everyday life, pointed out a central truth that called out an intended response from the listeners. On one occasion Jesus told three parables in response to the self-righteous complaints of the Pharisees and teachers of the law about the company Jesus kept.

Now the tax collectors and sinners were all gathering around to hear Jesus. But the Pharisees and the teachers of the law muttered, "This man welcomes sinners and eats with them."

Then Jesus told them this parable: "Suppose one of you has a hundred sheep and loses one of them. Doesn't he leave the ninety-nine in the open country and go after the lost sheep until he finds it? And when he finds it, he joyfully puts it on his shoulders and goes home. Then he calls his friends and neighbors together and says, 'Rejoice with me; I have found my lost sheep.' I tell you that in the same way there will be more rejoicing in heaven over one sinner who repents than over ninety-nine righteous persons who do not need to repent.

"Or suppose a woman has ten silver coins and loses one. Doesn't she light a lamp, sweep the house and search carefully until she finds it? And when she finds it, she calls her friends and neighbors together and says, 'Rejoice with me; I have found my lost coin.' In the same way, I tell you, there is rejoicing in the presence of the angels of God over one sinner who repents."

Jesus continued: "There was a man who had two sons. The younger one said to his father, 'Father, give me my share of the estate.' So he divided his property between them.

"Not long after that, the younger son got together all he had, set off for a distant country and there squandered his wealth in wild living. After he had spent everything, there was a severe famine in that whole country, and he began to be in need. So he went and hired himself out to a citizen of that country, who sent him to his fields to feed pigs. He longed to fill his stomach with the pods that the pigs were eating, but no one gave him anything.

"When he came to his senses, he said, 'How many of my father's hired servants have food to spare, and here I am starving to death! I will set out and go back to my father and say to him: Father, I have sinned against heaven and against you. I am no longer worthy to be called your son; make me like one of your hired servants.' So he got up and went to his father.

"But while he was still a long way off, his father saw him and was filled with compassion for him; he ran to his son, threw his arms around him and kissed him.

"The son said to him, 'Father, I have sinned against heaven and against you. I am no longer worthy to be called your son.'

"But the father said to his servants, 'Quick! Bring the best robe and put it on him. Put a ring on his finger and sandals on his feet. Bring the fattened calf and kill it. Let's have a feast and celebrate. For this son of mine was dead and is alive again; he was lost and is found.' So they began to celebrate.

"Meanwhile, the older son was in the field. When he came near the house, he heard music and dancing. So he called one of the servants and asked him what was going on. 'Your brother has come,' he replied, 'and your father has killed the fattened calf because he has him back safe and sound.'

"The older brother became angry and refused to go in. So his father went out and pleaded with him. But he answered his father, 'Look! All these years I've been slaving for you and never disobeyed your orders. Yet you never gave me even a young goat so I could celebrate with my friends. But when this son of yours who has squandered your property with prostitutes comes home, you kill the fattened calf for him!'

"'My son,' the father said, 'you are always with me, and everything I have is yours. But we had to celebrate and be glad, because this brother of yours was dead and is alive again; he was lost and is found.'"

Another time Jesus used a parable when he was questioned by a religious leader.

On one occasion an expert in the law stood up to test Jesus. "Teacher," he asked, "what must I do to inherit eternal life?"

"What is written in the Law?" he replied. "How do you read it?"

He answered, "'Love the Lord your God with all your heart and with all your soul and with all your strength and with all your mind'; and, 'Love your neighbor as yourself.'"

"You have answered correctly," Jesus replied. "Do this and you will live."

But he wanted to justify himself, so he asked Jesus, "And who is my neighbor?"

In reply Jesus said: "A man was going down from Jerusalem to Jericho, when he was attacked by robbers. They stripped him of his clothes, beat him and went away, leaving him half dead. A priest happened to be going down the same road, and when he saw the man, he passed by on the other side. So too, a Levite, when he came to the place and saw him, passed by on the other side. But a Samaritan, as he traveled, came where the man was; and when he saw him, he took pity on him. He went to him and bandaged his wounds, pouring on oil and wine. Then he put the man on his own donkey, brought him to an inn and took care of him. The next day he took out two denarii[1] and gave them to the innkeeper. 'Look after him,' he said, 'and when I return, I will reimburse you for any extra expense you may have.'

---

[1] **Denarii:** A denarius was the daily wage of a day laborer.

"Which of these three do you think was a neighbor to the man who fell into the hands of robbers?"

The expert in the law replied, "The one who had mercy on him."

Jesus told him, "Go and do likewise."

Besides teaching in parables, Jesus also taught in a more direct style, as seen in what came to be known as the "Sermon on the Mount."

Now when Jesus saw the crowds, he went up on a mountainside and sat down. His disciples came to him, and he began to teach them.

He said:

> "Blessed are the poor in spirit,
>   for theirs is the kingdom of heaven.
> Blessed are those who mourn,
>   for they will be comforted.
> Blessed are the meek,
>   for they will inherit the earth.
> Blessed are those who hunger and thirst for righteousness,
>   for they will be filled.
> Blessed are the merciful,
>   for they will be shown mercy.
> Blessed are the pure in heart,
>   for they will see God.
> Blessed are the peacemakers,
>   for they will be called children of God.
> Blessed are those who are persecuted because of righteousness,
>   for theirs is the kingdom of heaven.

"Blessed are you when people insult you, persecute you and falsely say all kinds of evil against you because of me. Rejoice and be glad, because great is your reward in heaven, for in the same way they persecuted the prophets who were before you.

"You are the salt of the earth. But if the salt loses its saltiness, how can it be made salty again? It is no longer good for anything, except to be thrown out and trampled underfoot.

"You are the light of the world. A town built on a hill cannot be hidden. Neither do people light a lamp and put it under a bowl. Instead they put it on its stand, and it gives light to everyone in the house. In the same way, let your light shine before others, that they may see your good deeds and glorify your Father in heaven.

"And when you pray, do not be like the hypocrites, for they love to pray standing in the synagogues and on the street corners to be seen by others. Truly I tell you, they have received their reward in full. But when you pray, go into your room, close the door and pray to your Father, who is unseen. Then your Father, who sees what is done in secret, will reward you. And when you pray, do not keep on babbling like pagans, for they think they will be heard because of their many words. Do not be like them, for your Father knows what you need before you ask him.

"This, then, is how you should pray:

"'Our Father in heaven,
hallowed be your name,
your kingdom come,
your will be done,
    on earth as it is in heaven.
Give us today our daily bread.
And forgive us our debts,
    as we also have forgiven our debtors.
And lead us not into temptation,
    but deliver us from the evil one.'

For if you forgive other people when they sin against you, your heavenly Father will also forgive you. But if you do not forgive others their sins, your Father will not forgive your sins.

"Do not store up for yourselves treasures on earth, where moths and vermin destroy, and where thieves break in and steal. But store up for yourselves treasures in heaven, where moths and vermin do not destroy, and where thieves do not break in and steal. For where your treasure is, there your heart will be also.

"The eye is the lamp of the body. If your eyes are healthy, your whole body will be full of light. But if your eyes are unhealthy, your whole body will be full of darkness. If then the light within you is darkness, how great is that darkness!

"No one can serve two masters. Either you will hate the one and love the other, or you will be devoted to the one and despise the other. You cannot serve both God and money.

"Therefore I tell you, do not worry about your life, what you will eat or drink; or about your body, what you will wear. Is not life more than food, and the body more than clothes? Look at the birds of the air; they do not sow or reap or store away in barns, and yet your heavenly Father feeds them. Are you not much more valuable than they? Can any one of you by worrying add a single hour to your life?

"And why do you worry about clothes? See how the flowers of the field grow. They do not labor or spin. Yet I tell you that not even Solomon in all his splendor was dressed like one of these. If that is how God clothes the grass of the field, which is here today and tomorrow is thrown into the fire, will he not much more clothe you—you of little faith? So do not worry, saying, 'What shall we eat?' or 'What shall we drink?' or 'What shall we wear?' For the pagans run after all these things, and your heavenly Father knows that you need them. But seek first his kingdom and his righteousness, and all these things will be given to you as well. Therefore do not worry about tomorrow, for tomorrow will worry about itself. Each day has enough trouble of its own.

"Therefore everyone who hears these words of mine and puts them into practice is like a wise man who built his house on the rock. The rain came down, the streams rose, and the winds blew and beat against that house; yet it did not fall, because it had its foundation on the rock. But everyone who hears these words of mine and does not put them into practice is like a foolish man who built his house on sand. The rain came down, the streams rose, and the winds blew and beat against that house, and it fell with a great crash."

Jesus' teachings moved many people and changed lives. However, those who continually heard his parables and sermons were his disciples. At one point during their travels together, the disciples' trust in Jesus was put to the test when a violent storm overtook their boat.

That day when evening came, he said to his disciples, "Let us go over to the other side." Leaving the crowd behind, they took him along, just as he was, in the boat. There were also other boats with him. A furious squall came up, and the waves broke over the boat, so that it was nearly swamped. Jesus was in the stern, sleeping on a cushion. The disciples woke him and said to him, "Teacher, don't you care if we drown?"

He got up, rebuked the wind and said to the waves, "Quiet! Be still!" Then the wind died down and it was completely calm.

He said to his disciples, "Why are you so afraid? Do you still have no faith?"

They were terrified and asked each other, "Who is this? Even the wind and the waves obey him!"

They went across the lake to the region of the Gerasenes. When Jesus got out of the boat, a man with an impure spirit came from the tombs to meet him. This man lived in the tombs, and no one could bind him anymore, not even with a chain. For he had often been chained hand and foot, but he tore the chains apart and broke the irons on his feet. No one was strong enough to subdue him. Night and day among the tombs and in the hills he would cry out and cut himself with stones.

When he saw Jesus from a distance, he ran and fell on his knees in front of him. He shouted at the top of his voice, "What do you want with me, Jesus, Son of the Most High God? In God's name don't torture me!" For Jesus had said to him, "Come out of this man, you impure spirit!"

Then Jesus asked him, "What is your name?"

"My name is Legion," he replied, "for we are many." And he begged Jesus again and again not to send them out of the area.

A large herd of pigs was feeding on the nearby hillside. The demons begged Jesus, "Send us among the pigs; allow us to go into them." He gave them permission, and the impure spirits came out and went into the pigs. The herd, about two thousand in number, rushed down the steep bank into the lake and were drowned.

Those tending the pigs ran off and reported this in the town and countryside, and the people went out to see what had happened. When they came to Jesus, they saw the man who had been possessed by the legion of demons, sitting there, dressed and in his right mind; and they were afraid. Those who had seen it told the people what had happened to the demon-possessed man — and told about the pigs as well. Then the people began to plead with Jesus to leave their region.

As Jesus was getting into the boat, the man who had been demon-possessed begged to go with him. Jesus did not let him, but said, "Go home to your own people and tell them how much the Lord has done for you, and how he has had mercy on you." So the man went away and began to tell in the Decapolis how much Jesus had done for him. And all the people were amazed.

When Jesus had again crossed over by boat to the other side of the lake, a large crowd gathered around him while he was by the lake. Then one of the synagogue leaders, named Jairus, came, and when he saw Jesus, he fell at his feet. He pleaded earnestly with him, "My little daughter is dying. Please come and put your hands on her so that she will be healed and live." So Jesus went with him.

A large crowd followed and pressed around him. And a woman was there who had been subject to bleeding for twelve years. She had suffered a great deal under the care of many doctors and had spent all she had, yet instead of getting better she grew worse. When she heard about Jesus, she came up behind him in the crowd and touched his cloak, because she thought, "If I just touch his clothes, I will be healed." Immediately her bleeding stopped and she felt in her body that she was freed from her suffering.

At once Jesus realized that power had gone out from him. He turned around in the crowd and asked, "Who touched my clothes?"

"You see the people crowding against you," his disciples answered, "and yet you can ask, 'Who touched me?'"

But Jesus kept looking around to see who had done it. Then the woman, knowing what had happened to her, came and fell at his feet and, trembling with fear, told him the whole truth. He said to her, "Daughter, your faith has healed you. Go in peace and be freed from your suffering."

While Jesus was still speaking, some people came from the house of Jairus, the synagogue leader. "Your daughter is dead," they said. "Why bother the teacher anymore?"

Overhearing what they said, Jesus told him, "Don't be afraid; just believe."

He did not let anyone follow him except Peter, James and John the brother of James. When they came to the home of the synagogue leader, Jesus saw a commotion, with people crying and wailing loudly. He went in and said to them, "Why all this commotion and wailing? The child is not dead but asleep." But they laughed at him.

After he put them all out, he took the child's father and mother and the disciples who were with him, and went in where the child was. He took her by the hand and said to her, "*Talitha koum!*" (which means "Little girl,

I say to you, get up!"). Immediately the girl stood up and began to walk around (she was twelve years old). At this they were completely astonished. He gave strict orders not to let anyone know about this, and told them to give her something to eat.

As Jesus went on from there, two blind men followed him, calling out, "Have mercy on us, Son of David!"

When he had gone indoors, the blind men came to him, and he asked them, "Do you believe that I am able to do this?"

"Yes, Lord," they replied.

Then he touched their eyes and said, "According to your faith let it be done to you"; and their sight was restored. Jesus warned them sternly, "See that no one knows about this." But they went out and spread the news about him all over that region.

While they were going out, a man who was demon-possessed and could not talk was brought to Jesus. And when the demon was driven out, the man who had been mute spoke. The crowd was amazed and said, "Nothing like this has ever been seen in Israel."

But the Pharisees said, "It is by the prince of demons that he drives out demons."

Jesus commissioned his closest followers, the 12 disciples, to spread out and tell people that the kingdom of God had come. He also gave them spiritual authority to heal people from sickness and demonic oppression.

This first band of preachers was sent out with almost no supplies in order to learn about faith and prayer. God performed many miracles through them, adding to the mounting excitement among the populace. A top official also heard the reports ... filtered through his guilty conscience.

King Herod heard about this, for Jesus' name had become well known. Some were saying, "John the Baptist has been raised from the dead, and that is why miraculous powers are at work in him."

Others said, "He is Elijah."

And still others claimed, "He is a prophet, like one of the prophets of long ago."

But when Herod heard this, he said, "John, whom I beheaded, has been raised from the dead!"

For Herod himself had given orders to have John arrested, and he had him bound and put in prison. He did this because of Herodias, his brother Philip's wife, whom he had married. For John had been saying to Herod, "It is not lawful for you to have your brother's wife." So Herodias nursed a grudge against John and wanted to kill him. But she was not able to, because Herod feared John and protected him, knowing him to be a righteous and holy man. When Herod heard John, he was greatly puzzled; yet he liked to listen to him.

Finally the opportune time came. On his birthday Herod gave a banquet for his high officials and military commanders and the leading men of Galilee. When the daughter of Herodias came in and danced, she pleased Herod and his dinner guests.

The king said to the girl, "Ask me for anything you want, and I'll give it to you." And he promised her with an oath, "Whatever you ask I will give you, up to half my kingdom."

She went out and said to her mother, "What shall I ask for?"

"The head of John the Baptist," she answered.

At once the girl hurried in to the king with the request: "I want you to give me right now the head of John the Baptist on a platter."

The king was greatly distressed, but because of his oaths and his dinner guests, he did not want to refuse her. So he immediately sent an executioner with orders to bring John's head. The man went, beheaded John in the prison, and brought back his head on a platter. He presented it to the girl, and she gave it to her mother. On hearing of this, John's disciples came and took his body and laid it in a tomb.

The apostles gathered around Jesus and reported to him all they had done and taught. Then, because so many people were coming and going that they did not even have a chance to eat, he said to them, "Come with me by yourselves to a quiet place and get some rest."

So they went away by themselves in a boat to a solitary place. But many who saw them leaving recognized them and ran on foot from all the towns and got there ahead of them. When Jesus landed and saw a large crowd, he had compassion on them, because they were like sheep without a shepherd. So he began teaching them many things.

By this time it was late in the day, so his disciples came to him. "This is a remote place," they said, "and it's already very late. Send the people away so that they can go to the surrounding countryside and villages and buy themselves something to eat."

But he answered, "You give them something to eat."

They said to him, "That would take more than half a year's wages! Are we to go and spend that much on bread and give it to them to eat?"

"How many loaves do you have?" he asked. "Go and see."

When they found out, they said, "Five — and two fish."

Then Jesus directed them to have all the people sit down in groups on the green grass. So they sat down in groups of hundreds and fifties. Taking the five loaves and the two fish and looking up to heaven, he gave thanks and broke the loaves. Then he gave them to his disciples to distribute to the people. He also divided the two fish among them all. They all ate and were satisfied, and the disciples picked up twelve basketfuls of broken pieces of bread and fish. The number of the men who had eaten was five thousand.

Immediately Jesus made the disciples get into the boat and go on ahead of him to the other side, while he dismissed the crowd. After he had dismissed them, he went up on a mountainside by himself to pray. Later that night, he was there alone, and the boat was already a considerable distance from land, buffeted by the waves because the wind was against it.

Shortly before dawn Jesus went out to them, walking on the lake. When the disciples saw him walking on the lake, they were terrified. "It's a ghost," they said, and cried out in fear.

But Jesus immediately said to them: "Take courage! It is I. Don't be afraid."

"Lord, if it's you," Peter replied, "tell me to come to you on the water."

"Come," he said.

Then Peter got down out of the boat, walked on the water and came toward Jesus. But when he saw the wind, he was afraid and, beginning to sink, cried out, "Lord, save me!"

Immediately Jesus reached out his hand and caught him. "You of little faith," he said, "why did you doubt?"

And when they climbed into the boat, the wind died down. Then those who were in the boat worshiped him, saying, "Truly you are the Son of God."

When they had crossed over, they landed at Gennesaret. And when the men of that place recognized Jesus, they sent word to all the surrounding country. People brought all their sick to him and begged him to let the sick just touch the edge of his cloak, and all who touched it were healed.

The next day the crowd that had stayed on the opposite shore of the lake realized that only one boat had been there, and that Jesus had not entered it with his disciples, but that they had gone away alone. Then some boats from Tiberias landed near the place where the people had eaten the bread after the Lord had given thanks. Once the crowd realized that neither Jesus nor his disciples were there, they got into the boats and went to Capernaum in search of Jesus.

When they found him on the other side of the lake, they asked him, "Rabbi, when did you get here?"

Jesus answered, "Very truly I tell you, you are looking for me, not because you saw the signs I performed but because you ate the loaves and had your fill. Do not work for food that spoils, but for food that endures to eternal life, which the Son of Man will give you. For on him God the Father has placed his seal of approval."

Then they asked him, "What must we do to do the works God requires?"

Jesus answered, "The work of God is this: to believe in the one he has sent."

So they asked him, "What sign then will you give that we may see it and believe you? What will you do? Our ancestors ate the manna in the wilderness; as it is written: 'He gave them bread from heaven to eat.'"

Jesus said to them, "Very truly I tell you, it is not Moses who has given you the bread from heaven, but it is my Father who gives you the true bread from heaven. For the bread of God is the bread that comes down from heaven and gives life to the world."

"Sir," they said, "always give us this bread."

Then Jesus declared, "I am the bread of life.[2] Whoever comes to me will never go hungry, and whoever believes in me will never be thirsty.

"Very truly I tell you, the one who believes has eternal life. I am the bread of life. Your ancestors ate the manna in the wilderness, yet they

---

[2] **Bread of life:** By saying this, Jesus was proclaiming that he is the source of true fulfillment and satisfaction.

died. But here is the bread that comes down from heaven, which anyone may eat and not die. I am the living bread that came down from heaven. Whoever eats this bread will live forever. This bread is my flesh, which I will give for the life of the world."

Then the Jews began to argue sharply among themselves, "How can this man give us his flesh to eat?"

Jesus said to them, "Very truly I tell you, unless you eat the flesh of the Son of Man and drink his blood, you have no life in you. Whoever eats my flesh and drinks my blood has eternal life, and I will raise them up at the last day. For my flesh is real food and my blood is real drink. Whoever eats my flesh and drinks my blood remains in me, and I in them. Just as the living Father sent me and I live because of the Father, so the one who feeds on me will live because of me. This is the bread that came down from heaven. Your ancestors ate manna and died, but whoever feeds on this bread will live forever."

From this time many of his disciples turned back and no longer followed him.

"You do not want to leave too, do you?" Jesus asked the Twelve.

Simon Peter answered him, "Lord, to whom shall we go? You have the words of eternal life. We have come to believe and to know that you are the Holy One of God."

Then Jesus replied, "Have I not chosen you, the Twelve? Yet one of you is a devil!" (He meant Judas, the son of Simon Iscariot, who, though one of the Twelve, was later to betray him.)

Jesus could get very personal, in-your-face, below the surface. He had a rock-solid sense of who he was, and he wanted his followers to know him to the core. Listening to his teaching and admiring his character were not enough. To follow this rabbi, his followers needed to know him in a deeper way, a way that would change their hearts, pursuits, and lives. He wanted to be the center, the joy, the "bread" and sustenance of their lives. As Jesus continued his ministry, he began to reveal more about who he was and why he had come.

—Includes portions of Matthew 5 – 7, 9, 14; Mark 4 – 6; Luke 10, 15; and John 6

Participant's Guide

Introduction

A pastor once had a man in his congregation who would from time to time approach him after the message and, with a twinkle in his eye, say, "Well, Pastor, as you got into your message today, the battery in my hearing aid died."

This was code for "I stopped listening when you hit on a topic (giving, holiness, humble service) that I did not want to hear." Apparently, the man had a bad case of Intentional Selective Hearing (ISH). Sadly, he missed out on truth that would have made his life better and drawn him closer to the Savior.

Even in Jesus' day the crowds, religious leaders, and sometimes the disciples themselves suffered from this sickness. They would ignore or even reject what Jesus said.

Two thousand years later, the teaching of Jesus can still be so piercing, convicting, and painfully true that we intentionally, or unintentionally, shut it off. As his followers, we must resist the occasional bout of ISH and cling to every word of the Savior ... even when those words challenge us to the core of our being.

Talk About It

Tell of a time when you read something in the Bible, heard a sermon, or had God bring a truth to your heart that you initially felt like rejecting or disobeying. What helped you finally come to a place where you accepted or embraced that truth?

Video Teaching Notes

As you watch the video segment for session 3, use the following outline to record anything that stands out to you.

I. Jesus is the Master Teacher

II. Jesus taught in parables

III. Jesus taught directly

IV. Jesus taught through life experiences

Video Discussion

1. What are some ways we can really tune in and open our hearts, ready to receive the truth God wants to speak in our life?

> *Jesus is the Master Teacher ... teaching us how to align our lives in the Lower Story according to God's Upper Story plan.*

2. In one of Jesus' most famous parables he used agricultural language and imagery to teach powerful spiritual truths (Mark 4:1 – 20; included in the session's Bible Reading). What are the four different kinds of soil in this parable and what do they represent?

   How can these same things still get in the way of people receiving God's truth and hearing his message?

3. Jesus told three parables about lost things that were found (Luke 15; included in the session's Bible Reading). What similar threads run through these stories and what do you learn about the love and heart of God from them?

4. Jesus taught with stories but also in more traditional messages, such as the Sermon on the Mount, where he called his followers to be salt and light (Matthew 5:13 – 16; included in the session's Bible Reading). What was he getting at with this challenge and how can we be salt and light in our daily lives?

5. Jesus taught his followers how to pray, the so-called "Lord's Prayer" (Matthew 6:9 – 15; included in the session's Bible Reading). This prayer was not given as a set of words to be repeated over and over with no thought to their meaning. Instead, each line was meant as a spring-board to lead us through key areas of concern. What themes does Jesus call us to include in our prayers and how can his words move us to a deeper place of prayer?

> *We are hungry, need daily bread,*
> *hold grudges, and experience stumbles*
> *into temptation. This is the Lower Story.*
> *So, we cry out to God to meet us in*
> *our Lower Story, and he does.*

6. Randy noted a third way that Jesus taught: using real-life situations as occasions to communicate deep spiritual truth. Why are real-life situations a good way to teach, particularly for parents and grandparents?

7. What lesson did Jesus teach after Peter tried to walk on the water (Matthew 14:22 – 33; included in the session's Bible Reading), and how can we learn from this lesson today?

8. Jesus is the Master Teacher, and that makes every Christian a student. What is one area of your life in which you feel God wants you to become a humble student and receive the teaching of Jesus?

Closing Prayer

Using the Lord's Prayer to guide you, pray through these themes:

- Lift up God for who he is, in his holiness. Declare his many names.
- Pray that his kingdom will come.
- Pray that his will be done in your life and on earth.
- Ask for his provision of what you need — daily bread.
- Ask for forgiveness and for power to forgive others.
- Pray that he will deliver you from temptation and give strength to resist.
- Pray against the wiles and tactics of the devil.

Between Sessions

Personal Reflections

Some of the best lessons Christians learn come from godly older people who have simply taught us in the natural flow of life. This is exactly what God had in mind in Deuteronomy 6:4 – 9 when he told the people to talk about his truth with their children at home, as they were taking walks, in the morning and in the evening. Consider how you can naturally share the truth of God's Word in normal daily interactions with the next generation.

Personal Action

Jesus told stories about a lost coin, a lost sheep, and a lost son. In each case, when the lost thing was found, a celebration followed. The message is this: a person coming to faith in Jesus ignites a party in heaven. Plan a party with some Christian friends for the express purpose of celebrating the fact that you are followers of Jesus. Take turns sharing how God brought you to faith and the people he used in the process. You might want to read Luke 15 at the party.

Read for Next Session

Take time before your next small group to read the Bible Reading for session 4, "Jesus, the Son of God."

Jesus, the Son of God

Everyone seems to have a theory on who Jesus was . . . only Jesus has the real answer.

Bible Reading

Jesus and his disciples went on to the villages around Caesarea Philippi. On the way he asked them, "Who do people say I am?"

They replied, "Some say John the Baptist; others say Elijah; and still others, one of the prophets."

"But what about you?" he asked. "Who do you say I am?"

Peter answered, "You are the Messiah."

Jesus warned them not to tell anyone about him.

He then began to teach them that the Son of Man must suffer many things and be rejected by the elders, the chief priests and the teachers of the law, and that he must be killed and after three days rise again. He spoke plainly about this, and Peter took him aside and began to rebuke him.

But when Jesus turned and looked at his disciples, he rebuked Peter. "Get behind me, Satan!" he said. "You do not have in mind the concerns of God, but merely human concerns."

Then he called the crowd to him along with his disciples and said: "Whoever wants to be my disciple must deny themselves and take up their cross and follow me. For whoever wants to save their life will lose it, but whoever loses their life for me and for the gospel[1] will save it. What good is it for someone to gain the whole world, yet forfeit their soul? Or what can anyone give in exchange for their soul? If anyone is ashamed of me and my words in this adulterous and sinful generation, the Son of Man will be ashamed of them when he comes in his Father's glory with the holy angels."

After six days Jesus took with him Peter, James and John the brother of James, and led them up a high mountain by themselves. There he was transfigured before them. His face shone like the sun, and his clothes became as white as the light.

Two men, Moses and Elijah, appeared in glorious splendor, talking with Jesus. They spoke about his departure, which he was about to bring to fulfillment at Jerusalem.

---

[1] **Gospel:** The message that Jesus has come to reconcile humanity to God and that each individual can accept this undeserved gift and enter into a relationship with him; synonymous with *Good News*.

Peter said to Jesus, "Rabbi, it is good for us to be here. Let us put up three shelters — one for you, one for Moses and one for Elijah." (He did not know what to say, they were so frightened.)

While he was still speaking, a bright cloud covered them, and a voice from the cloud said, "This is my Son, whom I love; with him I am well pleased. Listen to him!"

When the disciples heard this, they fell facedown to the ground, terrified. But Jesus came and touched them. "Get up," he said. "Don't be afraid." When they looked up, they saw no one except Jesus.

As they were coming down the mountain, Jesus gave them orders not to tell anyone what they had seen until the Son of Man had risen from the dead. They kept the matter to themselves, discussing what "rising from the dead" meant.

When they came to the other disciples, they saw a large crowd around them and the teachers of the law arguing with them. As soon as all the people saw Jesus, they were overwhelmed with wonder and ran to greet him.

They left that place and passed through Galilee. Jesus did not want anyone to know where they were, because he was teaching his disciples. He said to them, "The Son of Man is going to be delivered into the hands of men. They will kill him, and after three days he will rise." But they did not understand what he meant and were afraid to ask him about it.

Remember King David and King Solomon? All the great kings of ancient Israel had been warriors, builders, and diplomats. Little wonder that most people, if they believed at all in a coming Messiah, imagined the new king would be the greatest warrior, builder, and deliverer of all. How odd, then, that Jesus seemed indifferent to regime change. His message was "Open your hearts to God." He did not gather a cache of weapons or train a commando platoon for toppling Roman rule. This unexpected focus, coupled with Jesus' insistence on genuine personal repentance, offended many in Jerusalem's religious establishment. Some educated Pharisees considered him a teacher of dangerous and misleading philosophy. In the midst of growing Jewish opposition and common-folk

*popularity, Jesus went to Jerusalem to celebrate one of the great-
est of the Jewish holidays, the Festival of Tabernacles. He used
the festival as a backdrop for revealing his authority, identity, and
mission.*

Now at the festival the Jewish leaders were watching for Jesus and asking, "Where is he?"

Among the crowds there was widespread whispering about him. Some
said, "He is a good man."

Others replied, "No, he deceives the people." But no one would say
anything publicly about him for fear of the leaders.

Not until halfway through the festival did Jesus go up to the temple
courts and begin to teach. The Jews there were amazed and asked, "How
did this man get such learning without having been taught?"

At that point some of the people of Jerusalem began to ask, "Isn't this
the man they are trying to kill? Here he is, speaking publicly, and they are
not saying a word to him. Have the authorities really concluded that he
is the Messiah? But we know where this man is from; when the Messiah
comes, no one will know where he is from."

Then Jesus, still teaching in the temple courts, cried out, "Yes, you
know me, and you know where I am from. I am not here on my own
authority, but he who sent me is true. You do not know him, but I know
him because I am from him and he sent me."

At this they tried to seize him, but no one laid a hand on him, because his
hour had not yet come. Still, many in the crowd believed in him. They said,
"When the Messiah comes, will he perform more signs than this man?"

On the last and greatest day of the festival, Jesus stood and said in a
loud voice, "Let anyone who is thirsty come to me and drink. Whoever
believes in me, as Scripture has said, rivers of living water will flow from
within them." By this he meant the Spirit, whom those who believed in
him were later to receive. Up to that time the Spirit had not been given,
since Jesus had not yet been glorified.

On hearing his words, some of the people said, "Surely this man is the
Prophet."

Others said, "He is the Messiah."

Still others asked, "How can the Messiah come from Galilee? Does not Scripture say that the Messiah will come from David's descendants and from Bethlehem, the town where David lived?" Thus the people were divided because of Jesus. Some wanted to seize him, but no one laid a hand on him.

When Jesus preached, he made many claims with which people took issue. He said he was the light—but only God himself is the source of light! He was from above—but only God claims residence in heaven! Jesus was setting out the clear and fateful choice: believe in him and know God's power in your life, or stay in spiritual darkness. This message would change everything.

When Jesus spoke again to the people, he said, "I am the light of the world. Whoever follows me will never walk in darkness, but will have the light of life."

The Pharisees challenged him, "Here you are, appearing as your own witness; your testimony is not valid."

Jesus answered, "Even if I testify on my own behalf, my testimony is valid, for I know where I came from and where I am going. But you have no idea where I come from or where I am going."

Once more Jesus said to them, "I am going away, and you will look for me, and you will die in your sin. Where I go, you cannot come."

This made the Jews ask, "Will he kill himself? Is that why he says, 'Where I go, you cannot come'?"

But he continued, "You are from below; I am from above. You are of this world; I am not of this world. I told you that you would die in your sins; if you do not believe that I am he, you will indeed die in your sins."

Even as he spoke, many believed in him.

To the Jews who had believed him, Jesus said, "If you hold to my teaching, you are really my disciples. Then you will know the truth, and the truth will set you free."

"Very truly I tell you, whoever obeys my word will never see death."

At this they exclaimed, "Now we know that you are demon-possessed!

Abraham died and so did the prophets, yet you say that whoever obeys your word will never taste death. Are you greater than our father Abraham? He died, and so did the prophets. Who do you think you are?"

Jesus replied, "If I glorify myself, my glory means nothing. My Father, whom you claim as your God, is the one who glorifies me. Though you do not know him, I know him. If I said I did not, I would be a liar like you, but I do know him and obey his word. Your father Abraham rejoiced at the thought of seeing my day; he saw it and was glad."

"You are not yet fifty years old," they said to him, "and you have seen Abraham!"

"Very truly I tell you," Jesus answered, "before Abraham was born, I am!" At this, they picked up stones to stone him, but Jesus hid himself, slipping away from the temple grounds.

There it was. Jesus told the crowd that he existed before Abraham was even born. He told the crowd that his life was without beginning. He told the crowd he was God! The crowd turned into a lynch mob. Advisers might have urged Jesus to give the religious leaders time to cool off, but Jesus would not be stopped. He was driven by a passion to show people the glory of God, and even when a close friend was ill and near death, he used that experience as another example of God's power.

Now a man named Lazarus was sick. He was from Bethany, the village of Mary and her sister Martha. (This Mary, whose brother Lazarus now lay sick, was the same one who poured perfume on the Lord and wiped his feet with her hair.) So the sisters sent word to Jesus, "Lord, the one you love is sick."

When he heard this, Jesus said, "This sickness will not end in death. No, it is for God's glory so that God's Son may be glorified through it." Now Jesus loved Martha and her sister and Lazarus. So when he heard that Lazarus was sick, he stayed where he was two more days, and then he said to his disciples, "Let us go back to Judea."

"But Rabbi," they said, "a short while ago the Jews there tried to stone you, and yet you are going back?"

Jesus answered, "Are there not twelve hours of daylight? Anyone who walks in the daytime will not stumble, for they see by this world's light. It is when a person walks at night that they stumble, for they have no light."

After he had said this, he went on to tell them, "Our friend Lazarus has fallen asleep; but I am going there to wake him up."

His disciples replied, "Lord, if he sleeps, he will get better." Jesus had been speaking of his death, but his disciples thought he meant natural sleep.

So then he told them plainly, "Lazarus is dead, and for your sake I am glad I was not there, so that you may believe. But let us go to him."

Then Thomas (also known as Didymus) said to the rest of the disciples, "Let us also go, that we may die with him."

On his arrival, Jesus found that Lazarus had already been in the tomb for four days. Now Bethany was less than two miles from Jerusalem, and many Jews had come to Martha and Mary to comfort them in the loss of their brother. When Martha heard that Jesus was coming, she went out to meet him, but Mary stayed at home.

"Lord," Martha said to Jesus, "if you had been here, my brother would not have died. But I know that even now God will give you whatever you ask."

Jesus said to her, "Your brother will rise again."

Martha answered, "I know he will rise again in the resurrection at the last day."

Jesus said to her, "I am the resurrection and the life. The one who believes in me will live, even though they die; and whoever lives by believing in me will never die. Do you believe this?"

"Yes, Lord," she replied, "I believe that you are the Messiah, the Son of God, who is to come into the world."

After she had said this, she went back and called her sister Mary aside. "The Teacher is here," she said, "and is asking for you." When Mary heard this, she got up quickly and went to him. Now Jesus had not yet entered the village, but was still at the place where Martha had met him. When the Jews who had been with Mary in the house, comforting her, noticed how quickly she got up and went out, they followed her, supposing she was going to the tomb to mourn there.

When Mary reached the place where Jesus was and saw him, she fell at his feet and said, "Lord, if you had been here, my brother would not have died."

When Jesus saw her weeping, and the Jews who had come along with her also weeping, he was deeply moved in spirit and troubled. "Where have you laid him?" he asked.

"Come and see, Lord," they replied.

Jesus wept.

Then the Jews said, "See how he loved him!"

But some of them said, "Could not he who opened the eyes of the blind man have kept this man from dying?"

Jesus, once more deeply moved, came to the tomb. It was a cave with a stone laid across the entrance. "Take away the stone," he said.

"But, Lord," said Martha, the sister of the dead man, "by this time there is a bad odor, for he has been there four days."

Then Jesus said, "Did I not tell you that if you believe, you will see the glory of God?"

So they took away the stone. Then Jesus looked up and said, "Father, I thank you that you have heard me. I knew that you always hear me, but I said this for the benefit of the people standing here, that they may believe that you sent me."

When he had said this, Jesus called in a loud voice, "Lazarus, come out!" The dead man came out, his hands and feet wrapped with strips of linen, and a cloth around his face.

Jesus said to them, "Take off the grave clothes and let him go."

Therefore many of the Jews who had come to visit Mary, and had seen what Jesus did, believed in him. But some of them went to the Pharisees and told them what Jesus had done. Then the chief priests and the Pharisees called a meeting of the Sanhedrin.

"What are we accomplishing?" they asked. "Here is this man performing many signs. If we let him go on like this, everyone will believe in him, and then the Romans will come and take away both our temple and our nation."

Then one of them, named Caiaphas, who was high priest that year, spoke up, "You know nothing at all! You do not realize that it is better for you that one man die for the people than that the whole nation perish."

He did not say this on his own, but as high priest that year he prophesied that Jesus would die for the Jewish nation, and not only for that nation but also for the scattered children of God, to bring them together and make them one. So from that day on they plotted to take his life.

Usually, people try to avoid trouble, yet Jesus set his direction straight toward those who were plotting to kill him. Jerusalem was the site of the Passover Festival celebration. People there needed to hear his message. Time was short. Jesus soon would enter Jerusalem for the last time.

People were bringing little children to Jesus for him to place his hands on them, but the disciples rebuked them. When Jesus saw this, he was indignant. He said to them, "Let the little children come to me, and do not hinder them, for the kingdom of God belongs to such as these. Truly I tell you, anyone who will not receive the kingdom of God like a little child will never enter it." And he took the children in his arms, placed his hands on them and blessed them.

As Jesus started on his way, a man ran up to him and fell on his knees before him. "Good teacher," he asked, "what must I do to inherit eternal life?"

"Why do you call me good?" Jesus answered. "No one is good — except God alone. You know the commandments: 'You shall not murder, you shall not commit adultery, you shall not steal, you shall not give false testimony, you shall not defraud, honor your father and mother.'"

"Teacher," he declared, "all these I have kept since I was a boy."

Jesus looked at him and loved him. "One thing you lack," he said. "Go, sell everything you have and give to the poor, and you will have treasure in heaven. Then come, follow me."

At this the man's face fell. He went away sad, because he had great wealth.

Jesus looked around and said to his disciples, "How hard it is for the rich to enter the kingdom of God!"

The disciples were amazed at his words. But Jesus said again, "Children, how hard it is to enter the kingdom of God! It is easier for a camel to go through the eye of a needle than for someone who is rich to enter the kingdom of God."

The disciples were even more amazed, and said to each other, "Who then can be saved?"

Jesus looked at them and said, "With man this is impossible, but not with God; all things are possible with God."

Then Peter spoke up, "We have left everything to follow you!"

"Truly I tell you," Jesus replied, "no one who has left home or brothers or sisters or mother or father or children or fields for me and the gospel will fail to receive a hundred times as much in this present age: homes, brothers, sisters, mothers, children and fields — along with persecutions — and in the age to come eternal life. But many who are first will be last, and the last first."

They were on their way up to Jerusalem, with Jesus leading the way, and the disciples were astonished, while those who followed were afraid. Again he took the Twelve aside and told them what was going to happen to him. "We are going up to Jerusalem," he said, "and the Son of Man will be delivered over to the chief priests and the teachers of the law. They will condemn him to death and will hand him over to the Gentiles, who will mock him and spit on him, flog him and kill him. Three days later he will rise."

When it was almost time for the Jewish Passover, many went up from the country to Jerusalem for their ceremonial cleansing before the Passover. They kept looking for Jesus, and as they stood in the temple courts they asked one another, "What do you think? Isn't he coming to the festival at all?" But the chief priests and the Pharisees had given orders that anyone who found out where Jesus was should report it so that they might arrest him.

How many times had Jesus instructed his followers to hold back, to not tell who he was, to wait? And they had waited. Now the waiting was over. As Jesus entered Jerusalem, he let the crowds rejoice. He knew what this week would hold, but for the moment, those who loved him could cheer and celebrate.

As they approached Jerusalem and came to Bethphage and Bethany at the Mount of Olives, Jesus sent two of his disciples, saying to them, "Go to the village ahead of you, and just as you enter it, you will find a colt tied there, which no one has ever ridden. Untie it and bring it here. If anyone asks you, 'Why are you doing this?' say, 'The Lord needs it and will send it back here shortly.'"

They went and found a colt outside in the street, tied at a doorway. As they untied it, some people standing there asked, "What are you doing, untying that colt?" They answered as Jesus had told them to, and the people let them go. When they brought the colt to Jesus and threw their cloaks over it, he sat on it. Many people spread their cloaks on the road, while others spread branches they had cut in the fields. Those who went ahead and those who followed shouted,

> "Hosanna!"[2]

> "Blessed is he who comes in the name of the Lord!"

> "Blessed is the coming kingdom of our father David!"

> "Hosanna in the highest heaven!"

When Jesus entered Jerusalem, the whole city was stirred and asked, "Who is this?"

The crowds answered, "This is Jesus, the prophet from Nazareth in Galilee."

Jesus entered the temple courts and drove out all who were buying and selling there. He overturned the tables of the money changers and the benches of those selling doves. "It is written," he said to them, "'My house will be called a house of prayer,' but you are making it 'a den of robbers.'"

The blind and the lame came to him at the temple, and he healed them. But when the chief priests and the teachers of the law saw the wonderful things he did and the children shouting in the temple courts, "Hosanna to the Son of David," they were indignant.

"Do you hear what these children are saying?" they asked him.

"Yes," replied Jesus, "have you never read,

> "'From the lips of children and infants
>   you, Lord, have called forth your praise'?"

And he left them and went out of the city to Bethany, where he spent the night.

Jesus spent much of his final week teaching at the temple. Rabbis commonly lectured in the temple or the synagogues. But this rabbi was different. This teacher changed everything by implying that the

---

[2] **Hosanna:** A Hebrew expression meaning *Save!* which became an exclamation of praise.

Messiah, the one greater even than David, was speaking to them. No one had talked like this before. No one had dared.

While Jesus was teaching in the temple courts, he asked, "Why do the teachers of the law say that the Messiah is the son of David? David himself, speaking by the Holy Spirit, declared:

"'The Lord said to my Lord:
  "Sit at my right hand
until I put your enemies
  under your feet."'

David himself calls him 'Lord.' How then can he be his son?"

The large crowd listened to him with delight.

The crowds liked Jesus, but the hatred of the religious leaders grew more intense. So human was Jesus that as his situation worsened, his heart was troubled. But Jesus faced his fear and refused to let it stop him from doing the will of God.

"Now my soul is troubled, and what shall I say? 'Father, save me from this hour'? No, it was for this very reason I came to this hour. Father, glorify your name!"

Then a voice came from heaven, "I have glorified it, and will glorify it again." The crowd that was there and heard it said it had thundered; others said an angel had spoken to him.

Jesus said, "This voice was for your benefit, not mine. Now is the time for judgment on this world; now the prince of this world will be driven out. And I, when I am lifted up from the earth, will draw all people to myself." He said this to show the kind of death he was going to die.

Even after Jesus had performed so many signs in their presence, they still would not believe in him.

Yet at the same time many even among the leaders believed in him. But because of the Pharisees they would not openly acknowledge their faith for fear they would be put out of the synagogue; for they loved human praise more than praise from God.

Then Jesus cried out, "Whoever believes in me does not believe in me only, but in the one who sent me. The one who looks at me is seeing the one who sent me. I have come into the world as a light, so that no one who believes in me should stay in darkness.

"If anyone hears my words but does not keep them, I do not judge that person. For I did not come to judge the world, but to save the world. There is a judge for the one who rejects me and does not accept my words; the very words I have spoken will condemn them at the last day. For I did not speak on my own, but the Father who sent me commanded me to say all that I have spoken. I know that his command leads to eternal life. So whatever I say is just what the Father has told me to say."

Now the Passover and the Festival of Unleavened Bread were only two days away, and the chief priests and the teachers of the law were scheming to arrest Jesus secretly and kill him. "But not during the festival," they said, "or the people may riot."

Behind the scenes, under the radar of politics or religious courts, a dark power was brewing and waiting. That evil power found an opening among Jesus' intimate circle of followers. Just a touch of greed was all that power needed to accelerate the plot.

Then Satan entered Judas, called Iscariot, one of the Twelve. And Judas went to the chief priests and the officers of the temple guard and discussed with them how he might betray Jesus. They were delighted and agreed to give him money. He consented, and watched for an opportunity to hand Jesus over to them when no crowd was present.

— Includes portions of Matthew 17, 21; Mark 8 – 12, 14;
Luke 9, 22; John 7 – 8, 11 – 12

Participant's Guide

Introduction

Sometime in the 1960s and '70s a new kind of thinking arose and specific language came with it. People started "trying to find themselves." Men and women would begin a personal quest to discover who they were. Young people would drop out of school so they could figure themselves out. Middle-agers, men in particular, would go through a midlife crisis, struggling with their identity and purpose.

Certainly in Jesus' day, most people did not have the luxury of "finding themselves." But they did enjoy coming up with theories about who Jesus was ... his true identity. The only one who was crystal clear about the answer to this question was Jesus himself. While people guessed, suggested, and made innuendos, Jesus waited for the right moment to declare publicly what he had known from before time.

Jesus always knew his identity and mission. At the right time, he made it clear, so that we would have the right answer to the question, "Who is Jesus?"

Talk About It

If you were to survey people walking down the street of a major city, what are some of the responses you would get to the question, "Who is Jesus?"

Video Teaching Notes

As you watch the video segment for session 4, use the following outline to record anything that stands out to you.

I. Jesus asks, "Who do people say I am?"

II. Peter responds

III. The religious leaders and others respond

IV. Jesus declares his true identity

Video Discussion

1. In an encounter with Peter, Jesus gave the Son of Man's job description (Mark 8:31 – 33; included in the session's Bible Reading). What things did Jesus say he would do and how did Peter respond? Why do you think Peter responded as he did?

   Jesus' response to Peter was very strong! What had Peter done wrong and how was Jesus' response an act of love?

2. Jesus told his followers they would do four things as they walked with him day by day: (1) deny self, (2) take up his cross, (3) follow him, and (4) be willing to lay down their lives for him and the gospel. What does it look like, in an ordinary day of your life, for you to seek to do these things?

3. God declared who Jesus is and what we are called to do in response (Matthew 17:5; included in the session's Bible Reading). In what ways can we live out this calling on a daily basis?

4. Human kings in the Bible (and in our world today) were exalted and received special honor. When Jesus walked on this earth he acted very differently. What contrasts do you see between how Jesus lived and how other kings live and behave?

5. When Jesus called himself the "light of the world," he assured his disciples that they would no longer walk in the dark if they followed him. How have you discovered the light of Jesus since you became a Christian and how does his presence keep you from living in the darkness?

6. As Jesus interacted with some of the religious elite he declared, "Before Abraham was born, I am!" (John 8:58; included in the session's Bible Reading). What was Jesus claiming and why did this upset the religious leaders so much that they wanted to kill him?

> *Jesus is the Lamb, without blemish, that died a million times in all those sacrifices in Israel. He is God. He is the Lamb of God offered up for our sins.*

7. Lazarus was sick, so his sisters sent word to Jesus (John 11; included in the session's Bible Reading). In this encounter Jesus declared that he was "the resurrection and the life." What was Jesus claiming about himself and why did it matter at that time and today?

8. Jesus is the Savior, Messiah, and Lamb of God. He came to live a sinless life, die on the cross in our place, and rise again in glory to break the power of sin and death. How does the truth of his identity clarify your life purpose and direction?

> *We now know God's full plan. He sent his Son, who sat by his side in the Upper Story to come down to the Lower Story to represent us. God's plan was for him to die. He paid for our sins so we could be made right with God and come back into a personal relationship with him like Adam and Eve had.*

Closing Prayer

As you take time to pray, here are some ideas to get you started:

- Pray for people in your community, nation, and the world to get a clear picture of who Jesus really is.
- Ask Jesus to set the course of your life direction based on who he is, not who you are.
- Declare that Jesus is the resurrection and the life and thank him for the hope of heaven that belongs to all who believe in him.

Between Sessions

Personal Reflections

Jesus came to be the perfect and final sacrifice for our sins. Reflect on what you have been saved from. Praise God for cleansing you of all sin because the Messiah, Jesus, paid the price in full.

Personal Action

As we walk through life we meet people who have all sorts of theories on who Jesus is. Make a commitment to read the Gospels (Matthew, Mark, Luke, and John) and keep a journal of all the things Jesus said about himself. Then ask the Holy Spirit to help you gently and graciously paint an accurate portrayal of Jesus to those people you encounter who have misconceptions about him.

Read for Next Session

Take time before your next small group to read the Bible Reading for session 5, "The Hour of Darkness."

The Hour of Darkness

His darkest hour led to our brightest!

Bible Reading

On the first day of the Festival of Unleavened Bread, when it was customary to sacrifice the Passover lamb, Jesus' disciples asked him, "Where do you want us to go and make preparations for you to eat the Passover?"

So he sent two of his disciples, telling them, "Go into the city, and a man carrying a jar of water will meet you. Follow him. Say to the owner of the house he enters, 'The Teacher asks: Where is my guest room, where I may eat the Passover with my disciples?' He will show you a large room upstairs, furnished and ready. Make preparations for us there."

The disciples left, went into the city and found things just as Jesus had told them. So they prepared the Passover.

When evening came, Jesus arrived with the Twelve.

Jesus knew that the hour had come for him to leave this world and go to the Father. Having loved his own who were in the world, he loved them to the end.

The evening meal was in progress, and the devil had already prompted Judas, the son of Simon Iscariot, to betray Jesus. Jesus knew that the Father had put all things under his power, and that he had come from God and was returning to God; so he got up from the meal, took off his outer clothing, and wrapped a towel around his waist. After that, he poured water into a basin and began to wash his disciples' feet, drying them with the towel that was wrapped around him.

He came to Simon Peter, who said to him, "Lord, are you going to wash my feet?"

Jesus replied, "You do not realize now what I am doing, but later you will understand."

"No," said Peter, "you shall never wash my feet."

Jesus answered, "Unless I wash you, you have no part with me."

"Then, Lord," Simon Peter replied, "not just my feet but my hands and my head as well!"

Jesus answered, "Those who have had a bath need only to wash their feet; their whole body is clean. And you are clean, though not every one of you." For he knew who was going to betray him, and that was why he said not every one was clean.

When he had finished washing their feet, he put on his clothes and returned to his place. "Do you understand what I have done for you?" he asked them. "You call me 'Teacher' and 'Lord,' and rightly so, for that is what I am. Now that I, your Lord and Teacher, have washed your feet, you also should wash one another's feet. I have set you an example that you should do as I have done for you. Very truly I tell you, no servant is greater than his master, nor is a messenger greater than the one who sent him. Now that you know these things, you will be blessed if you do them."

Jesus was troubled in spirit and testified, "Very truly I tell you, one of you is going to betray me."

His disciples stared at one another, at a loss to know which of them he meant. One of them, the disciple whom Jesus loved,[1] was reclining next to him. Simon Peter motioned to this disciple and said, "Ask him which one he means."

Leaning back against Jesus, he asked him, "Lord, who is it?"

Jesus answered, "It is the one to whom I will give this piece of bread when I have dipped it in the dish." Then, dipping the piece of bread, he gave it to Judas, the son of Simon Iscariot. As soon as Judas took the bread, Satan entered into him.

So Jesus told him, "What you are about to do, do quickly." But no one at the meal understood why Jesus said this to him. Since Judas had charge of the money, some thought Jesus was telling him to buy what was needed for the festival, or to give something to the poor. As soon as Judas had taken the bread, he went out. And it was night.

After Judas left, Jesus gave the disciples a glimpse of what was to come. He foreshadowed the fact that he was going to be "broken" and "poured out"—he was going to take humanity's punishment for sin on himself.

While they were eating, Jesus took bread, and when he had given thanks, he broke it and gave it to his disciples, saying, "Take and eat; this is my body."

Then he took a cup, and when he had given thanks, he gave it to them, saying, "Drink from it, all of you. This is my blood of the covenant, which is poured out for many for the forgiveness of sins. I tell you, I will not

---

[1] **Disciple whom Jesus loved:** Probably John.

drink from this fruit of the vine from now on until that day when I drink it new with you in my Father's kingdom."

Jesus warned his disciples that he would be with them only a little while longer. He went on to comfort his confused followers.

"Do not let your hearts be troubled. You believe in God; believe also in me. My Father's house has many rooms; if that were not so, would I have told you that I am going there to prepare a place for you? And if I go and prepare a place for you, I will come back and take you to be with me that you also may be where I am. You know the way to the place where I am going."

Thomas said to him, "Lord, we don't know where you are going, so how can we know the way?"

Jesus answered, "I am the way and the truth and the life. No one comes to the Father except through me. If you really know me, you will know my Father as well. From now on, you do know him and have seen him."

Philip said, "Lord, show us the Father and that will be enough for us."

Jesus answered: "Don't you know me, Philip, even after I have been among you such a long time? Anyone who has seen me has seen the Father. How can you say, 'Show us the Father'? Don't you believe that I am in the Father, and that the Father is in me? The words I say to you I do not speak on my own authority. Rather, it is the Father, living in me, who is doing his work. Believe me when I say that I am in the Father and the Father is in me; or at least believe on the evidence of the works themselves. Very truly I tell you, whoever believes in me will do the works I have been doing, and they will do even greater things than these, because I am going to the Father. And I will do whatever you ask in my name, so that the Father may be glorified in the Son. You may ask me for anything in my name, and I will do it.

"If you love me, keep my commands. And I will ask the Father, and he will give you another advocate to help you and be with you forever — the Spirit of truth. The world cannot accept him, because it neither sees him nor knows him. But you know him, for he lives with you and will be in you.

"I have much more to say to you, more than you can now bear. But when he, the Spirit of truth, comes, he will guide you into all the truth. He will not speak on his own; he will speak only what he hears, and he will tell you what is yet to come.

"A time is coming and in fact has come when you will be scattered, each to your own home. You will leave me all alone. Yet I am not alone, for my Father is with me.

"I have told you these things, so that in me you may have peace. In this world you will have trouble. But take heart! I have overcome the world."

After Jesus said this, he looked toward heaven and prayed:

"Father, the hour has come. Glorify your Son, that your Son may glorify you. For you granted him authority over all people that he might give eternal life to all those you have given him. Now this is eternal life: that they know you, the only true God, and Jesus Christ, whom you have sent. I have brought you glory on earth by finishing the work you gave me to do. And now, Father, glorify me in your presence with the glory I had with you before the world began.

"Father, I want those you have given me to be with me where I am, and to see my glory, the glory you have given me because you loved me before the creation of the world.

"Righteous Father, though the world does not know you, I know you, and they know that you have sent me. I have made you known to them, and will continue to make you known in order that the love you have for me may be in them and that I myself may be in them."

When they had sung a hymn, they went out to the Mount of Olives.

Perhaps they sang a hymn from Psalms 115 – 118, the traditional psalms sung as part of the Passover meal. "The LORD is gracious and righteous; our God is full of compassion ... Give thanks to the LORD, for he is good; his love endures forever ... Blessed is he who comes in the name of the LORD." What were the disciples thinking and feeling as they followed Jesus to the Mount of Olives? They had probably gone to this place with him many times before for prayer and conversation. But now, shadows too dark for them to comprehend were beginning to fall on their hopes and dreams.

Then Jesus told them, "This very night you will all fall away on account of me, for it is written:

"'I will strike the shepherd,
and the sheep of the flock will be scattered.'

But after I have risen, I will go ahead of you into Galilee."

Peter replied, "Even if all fall away on account of you, I never will."

"Truly I tell you," Jesus answered, "this very night, before the rooster crows, you will disown me three times."

But Peter declared, "Even if I have to die with you, I will never disown you." And all the other disciples said the same.

Then Jesus went with his disciples to a place called Gethsemane, and he said to them, "Sit here while I go over there and pray." He took Peter and the two sons of Zebedee along with him, and he began to be sorrowful and troubled. Then he said to them, "My soul is overwhelmed with sorrow to the point of death. Stay here and keep watch with me."

Going a little farther, he fell with his face to the ground and prayed, "My Father, if it is possible, may this cup be taken from me. Yet not as I will, but as you will."

Then he returned to his disciples and found them sleeping. "Couldn't you men keep watch with me for one hour?" he asked Peter. "Watch and pray so that you will not fall into temptation. The spirit is willing, but the flesh is weak."

He went away a second time and prayed, "My Father, if it is not possible for this cup to be taken away unless I drink it, may your will be done."

An angel from heaven appeared to him and strengthened him. And being in anguish, he prayed more earnestly, and his sweat was like drops of blood falling to the ground.

When he came back, he again found them sleeping, because their eyes were heavy. So he left them and went away once more and prayed the third time, saying the same thing.

Then he returned to the disciples and said to them, "Are you still sleeping and resting? Look, the hour has come, and the Son of Man is delivered into the hands of sinners. Rise! Let us go! Here comes my betrayer!"

While he was still speaking, Judas, one of the Twelve, arrived. With him was a large crowd armed with swords and clubs, sent from the chief priests and the elders of the people.

Jesus, knowing all that was going to happen to him, went out and asked them, "Who is it you want?"

"Jesus of Nazareth," they replied.

"I am he," Jesus said. (And Judas the traitor was standing there with them.) When Jesus said, "I am he," they drew back and fell to the ground.

Again he asked them, "Who is it you want?"

"Jesus of Nazareth," they said.

Jesus answered, "I told you that I am he. If you are looking for me, then let these men go." This happened so that the words he had spoken would be fulfilled: "I have not lost one of those you gave me."

Then Simon Peter, who had a sword, drew it and struck the high priest's servant, cutting off his right ear. (The servant's name was Malchus.)

Jesus commanded Peter, "Put your sword away! Shall I not drink the cup the Father has given me?"

And he touched the man's ear and healed him.

Then Jesus said to the chief priests, the officers of the temple guard, and the elders, who had come for him, "Am I leading a rebellion, that you have come with swords and clubs? Every day I was with you in the temple courts, and you did not lay a hand on me. But this is your hour — when darkness reigns."

Soldiers of the Jewish religious establishment had come to place Jesus under arrest, and Jesus gave himself up. He could topple his foes with a word. He had the power to call on vast armies of angels to rescue him, but instead he surrendered. The disciples knew something very bad was happening, and they ran away to save their own skins. Jesus was left alone with his captors.

Those who had arrested Jesus took him to Caiaphas the high priest, where the teachers of the law and the elders had assembled. But Peter followed him at a distance, right up to the courtyard of the high priest. He entered and sat down with the guards to see the outcome.

The chief priests and the whole Sanhedrin were looking for false evidence against Jesus so that they could put him to death. But they did not find any, though many false witnesses came forward.

Finally two came forward and declared, "This fellow said, 'I am able to destroy the temple of God and rebuild it in three days.'"

Then the high priest stood up and said to Jesus, "Are you not going to answer? What is this testimony that these men are bringing against you?" But Jesus remained silent.

The high priest said to him, "I charge you under oath by the living God: Tell us if you are the Messiah, the Son of God."

"You have said so," Jesus replied. "But I say to all of you: From now on you will see the Son of Man sitting at the right hand of the Mighty One and coming on the clouds of heaven."

Then the high priest tore his clothes and said, "He has spoken blasphemy! Why do we need any more witnesses? Look, now you have heard the blasphemy. What do you think?"

"He is worthy of death," they answered.

Then they spit in his face and struck him with their fists. Others slapped him and said, "Prophesy to us, Messiah. Who hit you?"

Peter was not the timid sort. His normal reaction to trouble was to wrestle it to the ground, not to run from it. Quite naturally, then, he was the one to follow the soldiers back to the high priest's house and wait for the outcome. Maybe he was dreaming up "Plan B" when a few people took him by surprise.

And when some there had kindled a fire in the middle of the courtyard and had sat down together, Peter sat down with them. A servant girl saw him seated there in the firelight. She looked closely at him and said, "This man was with him."

But he denied it. "Woman, I don't know him," he said.

A little later someone else saw him and said, "You also are one of them."

"Man, I am not!" Peter replied.

About an hour later another asserted, "Certainly this fellow was with him, for he is a Galilean."

Peter replied, "Man, I don't know what you're talking about!" Just as he was speaking, the rooster crowed. The Lord turned and looked straight at Peter. Then Peter remembered the word the Lord had spoken to him: "Before the rooster crows today, you will disown me three times." And he went outside and wept bitterly.

Early in the morning, all the chief priests and the elders of the people made their plans how to have Jesus executed. So they bound him, led him away and handed him over to Pilate the governor.

When Judas, who had betrayed him, saw that Jesus was condemned, he was seized with remorse and returned the thirty pieces of silver to the chief priests and the elders. "I have sinned," he said, "for I have betrayed innocent blood."

"What is that to us?" they replied. "That's your responsibility."

So Judas threw the money into the temple and left. Then he went away and hanged himself.

The Jewish leaders brought Jesus to Pilate, who had governed the region of Judea for Rome for four years. Historical records reveal that he was no friend of the Jews. He frequently ordered soldiers to beat and kill Jewish protestors, and he had no compunction about offending Jewish leaders by placing symbols of pagan Roman worship in Jerusalem. On this Friday morning of Passover week, the Jewish leaders asked him to judge Jesus as a subversive threat. Now Pilate was caught. If he refused to condemn Jesus, Jewish accusers would portray him as no friend of Caesar (a very dangerous public image). If he agreed to crucify Jesus, he'd be acting against his own judicial instincts and, perhaps worse, caving in to those he despised. He needed to question this prisoner himself.

Pilate then went back inside the palace, summoned Jesus and asked him, "Are you the king of the Jews?"

"Is that your own idea," Jesus asked, "or did others talk to you about me?"

"Am I a Jew?" Pilate replied. "Your own people and chief priests handed you over to me. What is it you have done?"

Jesus said, "My kingdom is not of this world. If it were, my servants would fight to prevent my arrest by the Jewish leaders. But now my kingdom is from another place."

"You are a king, then!" said Pilate.

Jesus answered, "You say that I am a king. In fact, the reason I was born and came into the world is to testify to the truth. Everyone on the side of truth listens to me."

"What is truth?" retorted Pilate. With this he went out again to the Jews gathered there and said, "I find no basis for a charge against him. But it is your custom for me to release to you one prisoner at the time of the Passover. Do you want me to release 'the king of the Jews'?"

They shouted back, "No, not him! Give us Barabbas!" Now Barabbas had taken part in an uprising.

Then Pilate took Jesus and had him flogged. The soldiers twisted together a crown of thorns and put it on his head. They clothed him in a purple robe and went up to him again and again, saying, "Hail, king of the Jews!" And they slapped him in the face.

Once more Pilate came out and said to the Jews gathered there, "Look, I am bringing him out to you to let you know that I find no basis for a charge against him." When Jesus came out wearing the crown of thorns and the purple robe, Pilate said to them, "Here is the man!"

As soon as the chief priests and their officials saw him, they shouted, "Crucify! Crucify!"

But Pilate answered, "You take him and crucify him. As for me, I find no basis for a charge against him."

The Jewish leaders insisted, "We have a law, and according to that law he must die, because he claimed to be the Son of God."

When Pilate heard this, he was even more afraid, and he went back inside the palace. "Where do you come from?" he asked Jesus, but Jesus gave him no answer. "Do you refuse to speak to me?" Pilate said. "Don't you realize I have power either to free you or to crucify you?"

Jesus answered, "You would have no power over me if it were not given to you from above. Therefore the one who handed me over to you is guilty of a greater sin."

From then on, Pilate tried to set Jesus free, but the Jewish leaders kept shouting, "If you let this man go, you are no friend of Caesar. Anyone who claims to be a king opposes Caesar."

When Pilate heard this, he brought Jesus out and sat down on the judge's seat at a place known as the Stone Pavement (which in Aramaic is Gabbatha). It was the day of Preparation of the Passover; it was about noon.

"Here is your king," Pilate said to the Jews.

But they shouted, "Take him away! Take him away! Crucify him!"

"Shall I crucify your king?" Pilate asked.

"We have no king but Caesar," the chief priests answered.

Finally Pilate handed him over to them to be crucified.

So the soldiers took charge of Jesus.

As they were going out, they met a man from Cyrene, named Simon, and they forced him to carry the cross.

Roman crucifixion was a cruel punishment. Nailed to a wooden cross by wrists and feet, it was an excruciating, slow, and very public way to die. The victim's groaning became a morning's entertainment for onlookers. Seeing the horrors of crucifixion was an effective deterrent for wrong-doers. For Jesus, this heinous death was undeserved. As he gave his life, he looked beyond it to God's bigger story of salvation that was being played out through his life and death.

Those who passed by hurled insults at him, shaking their heads and saying, "So! You who are going to destroy the temple and build it in three days, come down from the cross and save yourself!"

In the same way the chief priests and the teachers of the law mocked him among themselves. "He saved others," they said, "but he can't save himself! Let this Messiah, this king of Israel, come down now from the cross, that we may see and believe."

Two other men, both criminals, were also led out with him to be executed. When they came to the place called the Skull, they crucified him there, along with the criminals — one on his right, the other on his left. Jesus said, "Father, forgive them, for they do not know what they are doing." And they divided up his clothes by casting lots.

The people stood watching, and the rulers even sneered at him. They said, "He saved others; let him save himself if he is God's Messiah, the Chosen One."

The soldiers also came up and mocked him. They offered him wine vinegar and said, "If you are the king of the Jews, save yourself."

There was a written notice above him, which read: THIS IS THE KING OF THE JEWS.

One of the criminals who hung there hurled insults at him: "Aren't you the Messiah? Save yourself and us!"

But the other criminal rebuked him. "Don't you fear God," he said, "since you are under the same sentence? We are punished justly, for we are getting what our deeds deserve. But this man has done nothing wrong."

Then he said, "Jesus, remember me when you come into your kingdom."

Jesus answered him, "Truly I tell you, today you will be with me in paradise."

Near the cross of Jesus stood his mother, his mother's sister, Mary the wife of Clopas, and Mary Magdalene. When Jesus saw his mother there, and the disciple whom he loved standing nearby, he said to her, "Woman, here is your son," and to the disciple, "Here is your mother." From that time on, this disciple took her into his home.

For those made to suffer crucifixion, death itself was the only resolution. So Jesus waited that day, along with two other victims and a crowd of onlookers, for death to overcome him. Before that, however, a deeper pain was coming. A pain that went far beyond the nails in his feet and wrists, the labored breathing, or the "crown" of thorns puncturing his brow. God poured out humanity's rightful punishment for sin upon his Son. And even the physical elements trembled.

It was now about noon, and darkness came over the whole land until three in the afternoon, for the sun stopped shining. And the curtain of the temple was torn in two.

About three in the afternoon Jesus cried out in a loud voice, "*Eli, Eli, lema sabachthani?*" (which means "My God, my God, why have you forsaken me?").

When some of those standing there heard this, they said, "He's calling Elijah."

Immediately one of them ran and got a sponge. He filled it with wine vinegar, put it on a staff, and offered it to Jesus to drink. The rest said, "Now leave him alone. Let's see if Elijah comes to save him."

When he had received the drink, Jesus said, "It is finished." With that, he bowed his head and gave up his spirit.

At that moment the curtain of the temple was torn in two from top to bottom. The earth shook, the rocks split and the tombs broke open. The bodies of many holy people who had died were raised to life. They came out of the tombs after Jesus' resurrection and went into the holy city and appeared to many people.

When the centurion and those with him who were guarding Jesus saw the earthquake and all that had happened, they were terrified, and exclaimed, "Surely he was the Son of God!"

When all the people who had gathered to witness this sight saw what took place, they beat their breasts and went away. But all those who knew him, including the women who had followed him from Galilee, stood at a distance, watching these things.

— Includes portions of Matthew 26 – 27; Mark 14 – 15;
Luke 22 – 23; and John 13 – 14, 16 – 19

Participant's Guide

Introduction

No moment in all history depicts a greater contrast between the Upper and Lower Story. The final week of Jesus' life, in the Lower Story, was as dark as darkness gets. The Lord of Glory was betrayed and abandoned by his friends, rejected by the crowds, condemned by the religious community, scorned and mocked mercilessly. He experienced absolute relational and emotional darkness.

The one humbly born in a manger was strung up on a post and brutally beaten. He was forced to carry his own cross up the hill of the Skull. Then he was nailed to that Roman instrument of torture and suspended up in the air by his hands and feet — suffering one of the most intentionally painful deaths ever invented. He experienced physical darkness beyond description.

Finally, the sinless Lamb of God experienced the pitch-blackness of utter spiritual darkness. The one who knew no sin became sin; in our place he took the punishment, the just judgment, we deserved.

Strangely, this darkest of all moments was also the moment heavenly light broke through as never before. As Jesus suffered and died, our hope began, our redemption was won, and sin was crushed. The brilliant light of God's love was shining from the glory of the Upper Story into the darkness of our Lower Story ... and it changed everything.

Talk About It

Tell about a time you experienced relational, emotional, or spiritual darkness and how the light of God was still shining.

Video Teaching Notes

As you watch the video segment for session 5, use the following outline to record anything that stands out to you.

I. Jesus, the sinless Son of God, provides the way back to God

II. In the Lower Story they said, "He is finished!"

III. In the Upper Story Jesus said, "It is finished!"

IV. A new beginning

Video Discussion

1. As Jesus prepared for the Passover meal (a time laden with imagery of sacrificed lambs and shed blood) he did not stop teaching and showing his followers how to live (John 13:1 – 17; included in the session's Bible Reading). Describe the act of service Jesus offered his disciples (including Judas) and how they responded.

   How does our willingness to serve reveal Jesus' presence in our life and in the world? What is one unexpected act of service you can offer in the coming week?

2. Jesus was emphatically clear that he is the only way back to a restored relationship with the Father, the only path to heaven (John 14:6; included in the session's Bible Reading). How do some people (even Christians) push back on this exclusive claim of Jesus? Why is it important for us to embrace this clear teaching of the Savior?

3. Right before his arrest, Jesus took three of his friends and went to a garden to pray (Matthew 26:36 – 46; included in the session's Bible Reading). What do you learn about the love and power of God, contrasted with the weakness and need of people, as you read this account?

4. The religious leaders and the political leaders joined in a twisted tale of abuse and rejection (Matthew 26:57 – 67; 27:1 – 10; John 18:28 – 19:16; included in the session's Bible Reading). How did they treat Jesus and how did he respond?

> *When Jesus died, the leaders of the Lower Story proclaimed, "He is finished." But Jesus from the Upper Story said, "It is finished."*

5. Peter, one of Jesus' closest friends, vigorously denied that he even knew the Lord three times — even as Jesus watched on (Luke 22:54 – 62; included in the session's Bible Reading). How must this have felt to Jesus? What are ways we deny Jesus and act like we don't know him?

6. What do you learn about the heart of Jesus as he hung on the cross (Luke 23:32 – 43; John 19:25 – 27; included in the session's Bible Reading), interacting with those who crucified him, the thief who reached out to him, and his own mother?

7. One of the briefest, most powerful statements in all of *The Story* is when Jesus said, "It is finished." From a Lower Story perspective, what must people have thought when Jesus spoke these words? From an Upper Story spiritual reality, what was Jesus declaring and what does this mean for us?

8. Hebrews 10:19 – 22, the passage Randy read in the video segment, points out three things that happen when we enter a friendship with Jesus. How have you experienced (or how are you experiencing) one of these in your life?

   • We can draw near God with absolute confidence.

   • We no longer have a guilty conscience.

   • We live with a sense of being cleansed and pure.

What can we do on a daily basis to walk in an intimate and living friendship with God?

> *Through the shed blood of Christ, we now have direct access to God. The curse of Adam has been lifted for all who believe in Jesus as the Son of God, the Messiah. Finally the way back to God has come. The only thing left for us to do is to reach and receive it for ourselves.*

Closing Prayer

As you take time to pray, here are some ideas to get you started:

- Thank Jesus for loving you so much that he would experience utter darkness as your sins and judgment became his.
- Praise God for sending his Holy Spirit to be with us and in us. Ask the Spirit to fill you to overflowing.
- In the garden, Jesus told his followers to pray that they would not fall into temptation. Pray against the lures and enticements the enemy puts in your path.

Between Sessions

Personal Reflections

Read Hebrews 10:19 – 22 and meditate on the truth that God has opened the way for you to draw near him with confidence, that you can live with a clear conscience through the sacrifice of Jesus, and that you have been washed and cleansed. Rejoice in these truths.

Personal Action

The whole purpose of Jesus entering the Lower Story and offering himself as a sacrifice was to bring us back into relationship with God. Write a brief account of how the death of Jesus has personally changed your life. Then share this brief reflection with a friend or two, and maybe with your pastor.

Read for Next Session

Take time before your next small group to read the Bible Reading for session 6, "The Resurrection."

The Resurrection

Up to this point in history it could be said, "Out of death comes death."
Now a new message rings loud and clear, "Out of death comes life!"

Bible Reading

Now it was the day of Preparation, and the next day was to be a special Sabbath. Because the Jewish leaders did not want the bodies left on the crosses during the Sabbath, they asked Pilate to have the legs broken and the bodies taken down. The soldiers therefore came and broke the legs of the first man who had been crucified with Jesus, and then those of the other. But when they came to Jesus and found that he was already dead, they did not break his legs. Instead, one of the soldiers pierced Jesus' side with a spear, bringing a sudden flow of blood and water. The man who saw it has given testimony, and his testimony is true. He knows that he tells the truth, and he testifies so that you also may believe. These things happened so that the scripture would be fulfilled: "Not one of his bones will be broken," and, as another scripture says, "They will look on the one they have pierced."

Later, Joseph of Arimathea asked Pilate for the body of Jesus. Now Joseph was a disciple of Jesus, but secretly because he feared the Jewish leaders. With Pilate's permission, he came and took the body away. He was accompanied by Nicodemus, the man who earlier had visited Jesus at night. Nicodemus brought a mixture of myrrh and aloes, about seventy-five pounds. Taking Jesus' body, the two of them wrapped it, with the spices, in strips of linen. This was in accordance with Jewish burial customs. At the place where Jesus was crucified, there was a garden, and in the garden a new tomb, in which no one had ever been laid. Because it was the Jewish day of Preparation and since the tomb was nearby, they laid Jesus there.

The next day, the one after Preparation Day, the chief priests and the Pharisees went to Pilate. "Sir," they said, "we remember that while he was still alive that deceiver said, 'After three days I will rise again.' So give the order for the tomb to be made secure until the third day. Otherwise, his disciples may come and steal the body and tell the people that he has been raised from the dead. This last deception will be worse than the first."

"Take a guard," Pilate answered. "Go, make the tomb as secure as you know how." So they went and made the tomb secure by putting a seal on the stone and posting the guard.

Jesus died and was buried on Friday. The next day was the Jewish Sabbath, and a guard was posted to prevent any tampering with the body. Then on the first day of the week, Sunday, those who mourned Jesus came to pay their respects.

When the Sabbath was over, Mary Magdalene, Mary the mother of James, and Salome bought spices so that they might go to anoint Jesus' body. Very early on the first day of the week, just after sunrise, they were on their way to the tomb and they asked each other, "Who will roll the stone away from the entrance of the tomb?"

There was a violent earthquake, for an angel of the Lord came down from heaven and, going to the tomb, rolled back the stone and sat on it. His appearance was like lightning, and his clothes were white as snow. The guards were so afraid of him that they shook and became like dead men.

The angel said to the women, "Do not be afraid, for I know that you are looking for Jesus, who was crucified. He is not here; he has risen, just as he said. Come and see the place where he lay. Then go quickly and tell his disciples: 'He has risen from the dead and is going ahead of you into Galilee. There you will see him.' Now I have told you."

So the women hurried away from the tomb, afraid yet filled with joy, and ran to tell his disciples.

So Peter and the other disciple[1] started for the tomb. Both were running, but the other disciple outran Peter and reached the tomb first. He bent over and looked in at the strips of linen lying there but did not go in. Then Simon Peter came along behind him and went straight into the tomb. He saw the strips of linen lying there, as well as the cloth that had been wrapped around Jesus' head. The cloth was still lying in its place, separate from the linen. Finally the other disciple, who had reached the tomb first, also went inside. He saw and believed. (They still did not understand from Scripture that Jesus had to rise from the dead.) Then the disciples went back to where they were staying.

Now Mary[2] stood outside the tomb crying. As she wept, she bent over

---

[1] **The other disciple:** Probably John.
[2] **Mary:** That is, Mary Magdalene.

to look into the tomb and saw two angels in white, seated where Jesus' body had been, one at the head and the other at the foot.

They asked her, "Woman, why are you crying?"

"They have taken my Lord away," she said, "and I don't know where they have put him." At this, she turned around and saw Jesus standing there, but she did not realize that it was Jesus.

He asked her, "Woman, why are you crying? Who is it you are looking for?"

Thinking he was the gardener, she said, "Sir, if you have carried him away, tell me where you have put him, and I will get him."

Jesus said to her, "Mary."

She turned toward him and cried out in Aramaic, "Rabboni!" (which means "Teacher").

Jesus said, "Do not hold on to me, for I have not yet ascended to the Father. Go instead to my brothers and tell them, 'I am ascending to my Father and your Father, to my God and your God.'"

Mary Magdalene went to the disciples with the news: "I have seen the Lord!" And she told them that he had said these things to her.

Now that same day two of them were going to a village called Emmaus, about seven miles from Jerusalem. They were talking with each other about everything that had happened. As they talked and discussed these things with each other, Jesus himself came up and walked along with them; but they were kept from recognizing him.

He asked them, "What are you discussing together as you walk along?"

They stood still, their faces downcast. One of them, named Cleopas, asked him, "Are you the only one visiting Jerusalem who does not know the things that have happened there in these days?"

"What things?" he asked.

"About Jesus of Nazareth," they replied. "He was a prophet, powerful in word and deed before God and all the people. The chief priests and our rulers handed him over to be sentenced to death, and they crucified him; but we had hoped that he was the one who was going to redeem Israel. And what is more, it is the third day since all this took place. In addition, some of our women amazed us. They went to the tomb early this morning but didn't find his body. They came and told us that they had seen a vision of angels, who said he was alive. Then some of our companions went to the tomb and found it just as the women had said, but they did not see Jesus."

He said to them, "How foolish you are, and how slow to believe all that the prophets have spoken! Did not the Messiah have to suffer these things and then enter his glory?" And beginning with Moses and all the Prophets, he explained to them what was said in all the Scriptures concerning himself.

As they approached the village to which they were going, Jesus continued on as if he were going farther. But they urged him strongly, "Stay with us, for it is nearly evening; the day is almost over." So he went in to stay with them.

When he was at the table with them, he took bread, gave thanks, broke it and began to give it to them. Then their eyes were opened and they recognized him, and he disappeared from their sight. They asked each other, "Were not our hearts burning within us while he talked with us on the road and opened the Scriptures to us?"

They got up and returned at once to Jerusalem. There they found the Eleven and those with them, assembled together and saying, "It is true! The Lord has risen and has appeared to Simon." Then the two told what had happened on the way, and how Jesus was recognized by them when he broke the bread.

While they were still talking about this, Jesus himself stood among them and said to them, "Peace be with you."

They were startled and frightened, thinking they saw a ghost. He said to them, "Why are you troubled, and why do doubts rise in your minds? Look at my hands and my feet. It is I myself! Touch me and see; a ghost does not have flesh and bones, as you see I have."

When he had said this, he showed them his hands and feet. And while they still did not believe it because of joy and amazement, he asked them, "Do you have anything here to eat?" They gave him a piece of broiled fish, and he took it and ate it in their presence.

He said to them, "This is what I told you while I was still with you: Everything must be fulfilled that is written about me in the Law of Moses, the Prophets and the Psalms."

Then he opened their minds so they could understand the Scriptures. He told them, "This is what is written: The Messiah will suffer and rise from the dead on the third day, and repentance for the forgiveness of sins will be preached in his name to all nations, beginning at Jerusalem. You are witnesses of these things. I am going to send you what my Father has promised; but stay in the city until you have been clothed with power from on high."

Now Thomas (also known as Didymus), one of the Twelve, was not with the disciples when Jesus came. So the other disciples told him, "We have seen the Lord!"

But he said to them, "Unless I see the nail marks in his hands and put my finger where the nails were, and put my hand into his side, I will not believe."

A week later his disciples were in the house again, and Thomas was with them. Though the doors were locked, Jesus came and stood among them and said, "Peace be with you!" Then he said to Thomas, "Put your finger here; see my hands. Reach out your hand and put it into my side. Stop doubting and believe."

Thomas said to him, "My Lord and my God!"

Then Jesus told him, "Because you have seen me, you have believed; blessed are those who have not seen and yet have believed."

Afterward Jesus appeared again to his disciples, by the Sea of Galilee. It happened this way: Simon Peter, Thomas (also known as Didymus), Nathanael from Cana in Galilee, the sons of Zebedee, and two other disciples were together. "I'm going out to fish," Simon Peter told them, and they said, "We'll go with you." So they went out and got into the boat, but that night they caught nothing.

Early in the morning, Jesus stood on the shore, but the disciples did not realize that it was Jesus.

He called out to them, "Friends, haven't you any fish?"

"No," they answered.

He said, "Throw your net on the right side of the boat and you will find some." When they did, they were unable to haul the net in because of the large number of fish.

Then the disciple whom Jesus loved[3] said to Peter, "It is the Lord!" As soon as Simon Peter heard him say, "It is the Lord," he wrapped his

---

[3] **The disciple whom Jesus loved:** Probably John.

outer garment around him (for he had taken it off) and jumped into the water. The other disciples followed in the boat, towing the net full of fish, for they were not far from shore, about a hundred yards. When they landed, they saw a fire of burning coals there with fish on it, and some bread.

Jesus said to them, "Bring some of the fish you have just caught." So Simon Peter climbed back into the boat and dragged the net ashore. It was full of large fish, 153, but even with so many the net was not torn. Jesus said to them, "Come and have breakfast." None of the disciples dared ask him, "Who are you?" They knew it was the Lord. Jesus came, took the bread and gave it to them, and did the same with the fish. This was now the third time Jesus appeared to his disciples after he was raised from the dead.

When they had finished eating, Jesus said to Simon Peter, "Simon son of John, do you love me more than these?"

"Yes, Lord," he said, "you know that I love you."

Jesus said, "Feed my lambs."

Again Jesus said, "Simon son of John, do you love me?"

He answered, "Yes, Lord, you know that I love you."

Jesus said, "Take care of my sheep."

The third time he said to him, "Simon son of John, do you love me?"

Peter was hurt because Jesus asked him the third time, "Do you love me?" He said, "Lord, you know all things; you know that I love you."

Jesus said, "Feed my sheep. Very truly I tell you, when you were younger you dressed yourself and went where you wanted; but when you are old you will stretch out your hands, and someone else will dress you and lead you where you do not want to go." Jesus said this to indicate the kind of death by which Peter would glorify God. Then he said to him, "Follow me!"

Then the eleven disciples went to Galilee, to the mountain where Jesus had told them to go. When they saw him, they worshiped him; but some doubted. Then Jesus came to them and said, "All authority in heaven and on earth has been given to me. Therefore go and make disciples of all nations, baptizing them in the name of the Father and of the Son and of the Holy Spirit, and teaching them to obey everything I have commanded you. And surely I am with you always, to the very end of the age."

Jesus did many other things as well. If every one of them were written down, I suppose that even the whole world would not have room for the books that would be written.

But these are written that you may believe that Jesus is the Messiah, the Son of God, and that by believing you may have life in his name.

God had promised since Old Testament days that he would redeem and restore his people. He sent his Son, the Savior, who died and was raised to life so that people could be forgiven and brought into a relationship of peace and fellowship with God. What a story! But was Jesus' resurrection the end of the saga? What else could possibly happen? Luke, the author of the Gospel by that name, answers that question in his second work—the "Acts of the Apostles," better known simply as "Acts."

—Includes portions of Matthew 27–28; Mark 16; Luke 24; and John 19–21

Participant's Guide

Introduction

Do you remember playing with a jack-in-the-box as a child? You would turn a crank on the side of this small metal toy (usually as the tune "Here We Go 'Round the Mulberry Bush" kept time with your movement). As the song neared the end, you would slow your cranking and begin to wince. You knew what was coming. You had done this a hundred times before. But there was still a sense of odd anticipation.

All of a sudden, with a slight rotation of the crank, the top of the box would flip open with a loud snap, and a spring-loaded head would pop up. Every single time Jack popped out of the box, you would be startled. But then you would press Jack's head down, click the lid of the box shut, and begin cranking again.

As we read this portion of *The Story*, we watch the disciples respond with stunned amazement at the resurrection of Jesus. He had told them, repeatedly, that he would die and rise again on the third day. He had assured them that death could not hold him down. But when Jesus popped out of the grave, the disciples were as shocked as a child with a jack-in-the-box!

Talk About It

Tell about something you knew was going to happen, but were still surprised and amazed when it actually did.

Video Teaching Notes

As you watch the video segment for session 6, use the following outline to record anything that stands out to you.

I. The disciples feel the sting of the Lower Story

II. An empty tomb: he is risen

III. Resurrection appearances

IV. Jesus commissions his followers before returning to the Upper Story

Video Discussion

1. Tell about a person you were close with who has passed away. How is that person's life still impacting yours?

2. Mary stood outside the empty tomb weeping … until Jesus revealed himself to her (John 20:10 – 18; included in the session's Bible Reading). What did Jesus teach her about himself? Tell about a moment when your eyes were opened, with greater clarity, and you came to know Jesus in a deeper way than you had before that moment.

> *Jesus is not finished. He is alive. But his work is finished. The way has been made open for all people, all nations, just as he promised Abraham, to receive the blessing of eternal life with God.*

3. On the road to Emmaus the resurrected Jesus taught two men the truth of the Old Testament Scriptures (Luke 24:13 – 49; included in the session's Bible Reading). How does understanding the first part of *The Story* (the Old Testament) help us understand the rest of it (the New Testament)?

4. Thomas was not willing to believe Jesus was alive until he saw him with his own eyes (John 20:24 – 29; included in the session's Bible Reading). When Jesus revealed himself to Thomas, how did he seek to meet Thomas right where he was and help him move toward faith? How has God met you similarly?

5. The risen Jesus met the disciples while they were out fishing (John 21:1 – 19; included in the session's Bible Reading). How did Peter respond when he realized it was Jesus? What did Jesus do to restore Peter and set him back on course to live a life of service?

At the end of Jesus' interaction with Peter, he said, "Follow me!" the same words he spoke when he first called Peter. Tell how Jesus has called you to follow him and one way you are seeking to live out this calling.

6. Before Jesus ascended back to the Upper Story of heaven, he called his followers to specific tasks (Matthew 28:16 – 20; included in the session's Bible Reading). What did Jesus call them (and us) to do and what is God's part and our part in this mission?

7. Where in your life are you feeling the sting of Lower Story pain but also experiencing Upper Story joy? How does focusing on Jesus' resurrection and the assurance of our own bring hope and strength in life's tough times?

8. When we understand the message of *The Story* and enter a restored relationship with God, we want to share it with others. Who is one person you are praying will enter a relationship with Jesus and how are you seeking to reach out to him or her? How can your group members encourage you in this relationship and support you in prayer?

> *We will no longer have to stand before the gravesides of people we have loved and grieve with no hope. If they embrace this free gift of forgiveness for themselves, they too will not be finished. We will see each other again in the garden of God to come.*

Closing Prayer

As you take time to pray, here are some ideas to get you started:

- Thank God for people you love who have passed away but still influence your walk of faith because of their great example.
- After the resurrection some people had a hard time recognizing Jesus. Ask the Holy Spirit to open your eyes to see Jesus with clarity.
- Pray that God will use you in his mission to make disciples of all nations.

Between Sessions

Personal Reflections

A Christian's funeral is filled with the hope and assurance of a glorious future. Not so for funerals of those who do not know Christ. Reflect on the people you love who do not have a relationship with Jesus. Invite God to direct how you might become more involved in their lives.

Personal Action

Create a list of the people you love and care about who have not discovered the truth of God's story and who are not yet in a relationship with God through faith in Jesus. Commit to use this list as a prayer reminder. Also, seek opportunities to share God's story and your story with them. Consider giving them a copy of *The Story* and encourage them to read it.

Read for Next Session

Take time before your next small group to read the Bible Reading for session 7, "New Beginnings."

New Beginnings

The human heart longs for a fresh start and a new vision. In Jesus we have received the new beginning our souls long for.

Bible Reading

In my former book, Theophilus, I wrote about all that Jesus began to do and to teach until the day he was taken up to heaven, after giving instructions through the Holy Spirit to the apostles he had chosen. After his suffering, he presented himself to them and gave many convincing proofs that he was alive. He appeared to them over a period of forty days and spoke about the kingdom of God. On one occasion, while he was eating with them, he gave them this command: "Do not leave Jerusalem, but wait for the gift my Father promised, which you have heard me speak about. For John baptized with water, but in a few days you will be baptized with the Holy Spirit."

Then they gathered around him and asked him, "Lord, are you at this time going to restore the kingdom to Israel?"

He said to them: "It is not for you to know the times or dates the Father has set by his own authority. But you will receive power when the Holy Spirit comes on you; and you will be my witnesses in Jerusalem, and in all Judea and Samaria, and to the ends of the earth."

After he said this, he was taken up before their very eyes, and a cloud hid him from their sight.

They were looking intently up into the sky as he was going, when suddenly two men dressed in white stood beside them. "Men of Galilee," they said, "why do you stand here looking into the sky? This same Jesus, who has been taken from you into heaven, will come back in the same way you have seen him go into heaven."

Jesus' ascension occurred 40 days after his resurrection. In the Jewish calendar, the harvest festival called Pentecost[1] came 50 days after the Sabbath of Passover week—coinciding with Jesus' crucifixion and resurrection. At this eventful Pentecost celebration, the Holy Spirit appeared like flames over the disciples' heads and endued them with the Holy Spirit's power and a new sense of God-with-us. During the 10 days between Jesus' ascension to heaven and the Festival of Pentecost, the 11 disciples chose a replacement for Judas, and then spent most of their time praying and waiting

---

[1] **Pentecost:** The Jewish festival celebrated on the 50th day after Passover. Jesus' disciples were celebrating this festival in Jerusalem when God sent his Holy Spirit to empower them with new life and blessing.

*for Jesus' promise of the Holy Spirit to arrive. When the Holy Spirit
came, the house rocked.*

When the day of Pentecost came, they were all together in one place.
Suddenly a sound like the blowing of a violent wind came from heaven
and filled the whole house where they were sitting. They saw what seemed
to be tongues of fire that separated and came to rest on each of them.
All of them were filled with the Holy Spirit and began to speak in other
tongues as the Spirit enabled them.

Now there were staying in Jerusalem God-fearing Jews from every
nation under heaven. When they heard this sound, a crowd came together
in bewilderment, because each one heard their own language being
spoken. Utterly amazed, they asked: "Aren't all these who are speaking
Galileans? Then how is it that each of us hears them in our native language? Parthians, Medes and Elamites; residents of Mesopotamia, Judea
and Cappadocia, Pontus and Asia,[2] Phrygia and Pamphylia, Egypt and the
parts of Libya near Cyrene; visitors from Rome (both Jews and converts
to Judaism); Cretans and Arabs — we hear them declaring the wonders of
God in our own tongues!" Amazed and perplexed, they asked one another,
"What does this mean?"

Some, however, made fun of them and said, "They have had too much
wine."

Then Peter stood up with the Eleven, raised his voice and addressed
the crowd: "Fellow Jews and all of you who live in Jerusalem, let me explain this to you; listen carefully to what I say. These people are not drunk,
as you suppose. It's only nine in the morning! No, this is what was spoken
by the prophet Joel:

" 'In the last days, God says,
    I will pour out my Spirit on all people.
Your sons and daughters will prophesy,
    your young men will see visions,
    your old men will dream dreams.
Even on my servants, both men and women,
    I will pour out my Spirit in those days,
    and they will prophesy.

---

[2] **Asia:** That is, the Roman province by the same name.

I will show wonders in the heavens above
    and signs on the earth below,
       blood and fire and billows of smoke.
The sun will be turned to darkness
    and the moon to blood
       before the coming of the great and glorious day of the Lord.
And everyone who calls
    on the name of the Lord will be saved.'

"Fellow Israelites, listen to this: Jesus of Nazareth was a man accredited by God to you by miracles, wonders and signs, which God did among you through him, as you yourselves know. This man was handed over to you by God's deliberate plan and foreknowledge; and you, with the help of wicked men, put him to death by nailing him to the cross. But God raised him from the dead, freeing him from the agony of death, because it was impossible for death to keep its hold on him.

"God has raised this Jesus to life, and we are all witnesses of it. Exalted to the right hand of God, he has received from the Father the promised Holy Spirit and has poured out what you now see and hear.

"Therefore let all Israel be assured of this: God has made this Jesus, whom you crucified, both Lord and Messiah."

When the people heard this, they were cut to the heart and said to Peter and the other apostles, "Brothers, what shall we do?"

Peter replied, "Repent and be baptized, every one of you, in the name of Jesus Christ for the forgiveness of your sins. And you will receive the gift of the Holy Spirit. The promise is for you and your children and for all who are far off — for all whom the Lord our God will call."

With many other words he warned them; and he pleaded with them, "Save yourselves from this corrupt generation." Those who accepted his message were baptized, and about three thousand were added to their number that day.

They devoted themselves to the apostles' teaching and to fellowship, to the breaking of bread and to prayer. Everyone was filled with awe at the many wonders and signs performed by the apostles. All the believers were together and had everything in common. They sold property and possessions to give to anyone who had need. Every day they continued to meet together in the temple courts. They broke bread in their homes and ate together with glad and sincere hearts, praising God and enjoying the favor of all the people. And the Lord added to their number daily those who were being saved.

One day Peter and John were going up to the temple at the time of prayer — at three in the afternoon. Now a man who was lame from birth was being carried to the temple gate called Beautiful, where he was put every day to beg from those going into the temple courts. When he saw Peter and John about to enter, he asked them for money. Peter looked straight at him, as did John. Then Peter said, "Look at us!" So the man gave them his attention, expecting to get something from them.

Then Peter said, "Silver or gold I do not have, but what I do have I give you. In the name of Jesus Christ of Nazareth, walk." Taking him by the right hand, he helped him up, and instantly the man's feet and ankles became strong. He jumped to his feet and began to walk. Then he went with them into the temple courts, walking and jumping, and praising God. When all the people saw him walking and praising God, they recognized him as the same man who used to sit begging at the temple gate called Beautiful, and they were filled with wonder and amazement at what had happened to him.

While the man held on to Peter and John, all the people were astonished and came running to them in the place called Solomon's Colonnade. When Peter saw this, he said to them: "Fellow Israelites, why does this surprise you? Why do you stare at us as if by our own power or godliness we had made this man walk? The God of Abraham, Isaac and Jacob, the God of our fathers, has glorified his servant Jesus. You handed him over to be killed, and you disowned him before Pilate, though he had decided to let him go. You disowned the Holy and Righteous One and asked that a murderer be released to you. You killed the author of life, but God raised him from the dead. We are witnesses of this. By faith in the name of Jesus, this man whom you see and know was made strong. It is Jesus' name and the faith that comes through him that has completely healed him, as you can all see.

"Now, fellow Israelites, I know that you acted in ignorance, as did your leaders. But this is how God fulfilled what he had foretold through all the prophets, saying that his Messiah would suffer. Repent, then, and turn to God, so that your sins may be wiped out, that times of refreshing may come from the Lord, and that he may send the Messiah, who has been appointed for you — even Jesus.

The priests and the captain of the temple guard and the Sadducees[3] came up to Peter and John while they were speaking to the people. They were greatly disturbed because the apostles were teaching the people, proclaiming in Jesus the resurrection of the dead. They seized Peter and John and, because it was evening, they put them in jail until the next day. But many who heard the message believed; so the number of men who believed grew to about five thousand.

The next day the rulers, the elders and the teachers of the law met in Jerusalem. Annas the high priest was there, and so were Caiaphas, John, Alexander and others of the high priest's family. They had Peter and John brought before them and began to question them: "By what power or what name did you do this?"

Then Peter, filled with the Holy Spirit, said to them: "Rulers and elders of the people! If we are being called to account today for an act of kindness shown to a man who was lame and are being asked how he was healed, then know this, you and all the people of Israel: It is by the name of Jesus Christ of Nazareth, whom you crucified but whom God raised from the dead, that this man stands before you healed. Jesus is

> "'the stone you builders rejected,
>   which has become the cornerstone.'

Salvation[4] is found in no one else, for there is no other name under heaven given to mankind by which we must be saved."

When they saw the courage of Peter and John and realized that they were unschooled, ordinary men, they were astonished and they took note that these men had been with Jesus. But since they could see the man who had been healed standing there with them, there was nothing they could say. So they ordered them to withdraw from the Sanhedrin and then con-

---

[3] **Sadducees:** An upper-class group of Jewish leaders who oversaw the temple administration.

[4] **Salvation:** Rescue from death or destruction. In the biblical sense, the term *salvation* expresses the release from the debt of sin owed to God and the experience of never-ending life with him in heaven. Also relevant to earthly life, *salvation* can refer to the transformation of people's daily lives when they believe in Jesus.

ferred together. "What are we going to do with these men?" they asked. "Everyone living in Jerusalem knows they have performed a notable sign, and we cannot deny it. But to stop this thing from spreading any further among the people, we must warn them to speak no longer to anyone in this name."

Then they called them in again and commanded them not to speak or teach at all in the name of Jesus. But Peter and John replied, "Which is right in God's eyes: to listen to you, or to him? You be the judges! As for us, we cannot help speaking about what we have seen and heard."

After further threats they let them go. They could not decide how to punish them, because all the people were praising God for what had happened.

All the believers were one in heart and mind. No one claimed that any of their possessions was their own, but they shared everything they had. With great power the apostles continued to testify to the resurrection of the Lord Jesus. And God's grace was so powerfully at work in them all that there were no needy persons among them. For from time to time those who owned land or houses sold them, brought the money from the sales and put it at the apostles' feet, and it was distributed to anyone who had need.

The apostles performed many signs and wonders among the people. And all the believers used to meet together in Solomon's Colonnade. No one else dared join them, even though they were highly regarded by the people. Nevertheless, more and more men and women believed in the Lord and were added to their number. As a result, people brought the sick into the streets and laid them on beds and mats so that at least Peter's shadow might fall on some of them as he passed by. Crowds gathered also from the towns around Jerusalem, bringing their sick and those tormented by impure spirits, and all of them were healed.

Then the high priest and all his associates, who were members of the party of the Sadducees, were filled with jealousy. They arrested the apostles and put them in the public jail. But during the night an angel of the Lord opened the doors of the jail and brought them out. "Go, stand in the temple courts," he said, "and tell the people all about this new life."

At daybreak they entered the temple courts, as they had been told, and began to teach the people.

When the high priest and his associates arrived, they called together the Sanhedrin — the full assembly of the elders of Israel — and sent to the jail for the apostles. But on arriving at the jail, the officers did not find them there. So they went back and reported, "We found the jail securely locked, with the guards standing at the doors; but when we opened them, we found no one inside." On hearing this report, the captain of the temple guard and the chief priests were at a loss, wondering what this might lead to.

Then someone came and said, "Look! The men you put in jail are standing in the temple courts teaching the people." At that, the captain went with his officers and brought the apostles. They did not use force, because they feared that the people would stone them.

The apostles were brought in and made to appear before the Sanhedrin to be questioned by the high priest. "We gave you strict orders not to teach in this name," he said. "Yet you have filled Jerusalem with your teaching and are determined to make us guilty of this man's blood."

Peter and the other apostles replied: "We must obey God rather than human beings! The God of our ancestors raised Jesus from the dead — whom you killed by hanging him on a cross. God exalted him to his own right hand as Prince and Savior that he might bring Israel to repentance and forgive their sins. We are witnesses of these things, and so is the Holy Spirit, whom God has given to those who obey him."

When they heard this, they were furious and wanted to put them to death. But a Pharisee named Gamaliel, a teacher of the law, who was honored by all the people, stood up in the Sanhedrin and ordered that the men be put outside for a little while. Then he addressed the Sanhedrin: "Men of Israel, consider carefully what you intend to do to these men. Some time ago Theudas appeared, claiming to be somebody, and about four hundred men rallied to him. He was killed, all his followers were dispersed, and it all came to nothing. After him, Judas the Galilean appeared in the days of the census and led a band of people in revolt. He too was killed, and all his followers were scattered. Therefore, in the present case I advise you: Leave these men alone! Let them go! For if their purpose or activity is of human origin, it will fail. But if it is from God, you will not be able to stop these men; you will only find yourselves fighting against God."

His speech persuaded them. They called the apostles in and had them flogged. Then they ordered them not to speak in the name of Jesus, and let them go.

The apostles left the Sanhedrin, rejoicing because they had been counted worthy of suffering disgrace for the Name. Day after day, in the temple courts and from house to house, they never stopped teaching and proclaiming the good news that Jesus is the Messiah.

Growing movements create logistical nightmares. As hundreds, then thousands, said yes to following the resurrected Jesus, they gathered together, full of joy and needs. So who would run the errands, distribute food, clean the dishes and make sure everyone had name tags? For these important service jobs, the 12 apostles chose a small corps of servers, considered to be the first "deacons." Among them was a man described as "full of God's grace and power." His name was Stephen.

Now Stephen, a man full of God's grace and power, performed great wonders and signs among the people. Opposition arose, however, from members of the Synagogue of the Freedmen (as it was called) — Jews of Cyrene and Alexandria as well as the provinces of Cilicia and Asia — who began to argue with Stephen. But they could not stand up against the wisdom the Spirit gave him as he spoke.

Then they secretly persuaded some men to say, "We have heard Stephen speak blasphemous words against Moses and against God."

So they stirred up the people and the elders and the teachers of the law. They seized Stephen and brought him before the Sanhedrin. They produced false witnesses, who testified, "This fellow never stops speaking against this holy place and against the law. For we have heard him say that this Jesus of Nazareth will destroy this place and change the customs Moses handed down to us."

All who were sitting in the Sanhedrin looked intently at Stephen, and they saw that his face was like the face of an angel.

Then the high priest asked Stephen, "Are these charges true?"

Stephen's answer to this question came in the form of a Jewish history lesson about God's great story of redemption. Then Stephen spoke of the "Righteous One," Jesus.

"You stiff-necked people! Your hearts and ears are still uncircumcised. You are just like your ancestors: You always resist the Holy Spirit! Was there ever a prophet your ancestors did not persecute? They even killed those who predicted the coming of the Righteous One. And now you have betrayed and murdered him — you who have received the law that was given through angels but have not obeyed it."

When the members of the Sanhedrin heard this, they were furious and gnashed their teeth at him. But Stephen, full of the Holy Spirit, looked up to heaven and saw the glory of God, and Jesus standing at the right hand of God. "Look," he said, "I see heaven open and the Son of Man standing at the right hand of God."

At this they covered their ears and, yelling at the top of their voices, they all rushed at him, dragged him out of the city and began to stone him. Meanwhile, the witnesses laid their coats at the feet of a young man named Saul.

While they were stoning him, Stephen prayed, "Lord Jesus, receive my spirit." Then he fell on his knees and cried out, "Lord, do not hold this sin against them." When he had said this, he fell asleep.

And Saul approved of their killing him.

On that day a great persecution broke out against the church in Jerusalem, and all except the apostles were scattered throughout Judea and Samaria. Godly men buried Stephen and mourned deeply for him. But Saul began to destroy the church. Going from house to house, he dragged off both men and women and put them in prison.

Those who had been scattered preached the word wherever they went. Philip went down to a city in Samaria and proclaimed the Messiah there. When the crowds heard Philip and saw the signs he performed, they all paid close attention to what he said. For with shrieks, impure spirits came out of many, and many who were paralyzed or lame were healed. So there was great joy in that city.

Meanwhile, Saul was still breathing out murderous threats against the Lord's disciples. He went to the high priest and asked him for letters to the synagogues in Damascus, so that if he found any there who belonged to the Way, whether men or women, he might take them as prisoners to Jerusalem. As he neared Damascus on his journey, suddenly a light from heaven flashed around him. He fell to the ground and heard a voice say to him, "Saul, Saul, why do you persecute me?"

"Who are you, Lord?" Saul asked.

"I am Jesus, whom you are persecuting," he replied. "Now get up and go into the city, and you will be told what you must do."

The men traveling with Saul stood there speechless; they heard the sound but did not see anyone. Saul got up from the ground, but when he opened his eyes he could see nothing. So they led him by the hand into Damascus. For three days he was blind, and did not eat or drink anything.

In Damascus there was a disciple named Ananias. The Lord called to him in a vision, "Ananias!"

"Yes, Lord," he answered.

The Lord told him, "Go to the house of Judas on Straight Street and ask for a man from Tarsus named Saul, for he is praying. In a vision he has seen a man named Ananias come and place his hands on him to restore his sight."

"Lord," Ananias answered, "I have heard many reports about this man and all the harm he has done to your holy people in Jerusalem. And he has come here with authority from the chief priests to arrest all who call on your name."

But the Lord said to Ananias, "Go! This man is my chosen instrument to proclaim my name to the Gentiles and their kings and to the people of Israel. I will show him how much he must suffer for my name."

Then Ananias went to the house and entered it. Placing his hands on Saul, he said, "Brother Saul, the Lord — Jesus, who appeared to you on the road as you were coming here — has sent me so that you may see again and be filled with the Holy Spirit." Immediately, something like scales fell from Saul's eyes, and he could see again. He got up and was baptized, and after taking some food, he regained his strength.

Saul spent several days with the disciples in Damascus. At once he began to preach in the synagogues that Jesus is the Son of God. All those who heard him were astonished and asked, "Isn't he the man who raised havoc in Jerusalem among those who call on this name? And hasn't he come here to take them as prisoners to the chief priests?" Yet Saul grew more and more powerful and baffled the Jews living in Damascus by proving that Jesus is the Messiah.

After many days had gone by, there was a conspiracy among the Jews to kill him, but Saul learned of their plan. Day and night they kept close watch on the city gates in order to kill him. But his followers took him by night and lowered him in a basket through an opening in the wall.

When he came to Jerusalem, he tried to join the disciples, but they were all afraid of him, not believing that he really was a disciple. But Barnabas took him and brought him to the apostles. He told them how Saul on his journey had seen the Lord and that the Lord had spoken to him, and how in Damascus he had preached fearlessly in the name of Jesus. So Saul stayed with them and moved about freely in Jerusalem, speaking boldly in the name of the Lord. He talked and debated with the Hellenistic Jews, but they tried to kill him. When the believers learned of this, they took him down to Caesarea and sent him off to Tarsus.

Then the church throughout Judea, Galilee and Samaria enjoyed a time of peace and was strengthened. Living in the fear of the Lord and encouraged by the Holy Spirit, it increased in numbers.

Most of the new Christians were Jewish, but God's story of Good News was for everyone. Things had to change.

At Caesarea there was a man named Cornelius, a centurion in what was known as the Italian Regiment. He and all his family were devout and God-fearing; he gave generously to those in need and prayed to God regularly. One day at about three in the afternoon he had a vision. He distinctly saw an angel of God, who came to him and said, "Cornelius!"

Cornelius stared at him in fear. "What is it, Lord?" he asked.

The angel answered, "Your prayers and gifts to the poor have come up as a memorial offering before God. Now send men to Joppa to bring back a man named Simon who is called Peter. He is staying with Simon the tanner, whose house is by the sea."

When the angel who spoke to him had gone, Cornelius called two of his servants and a devout soldier who was one of his attendants. He told them everything that had happened and sent them to Joppa.

About noon the following day as they were on their journey and approaching the city, Peter went up on the roof to pray. He became hungry and wanted something to eat, and while the meal was being prepared, he fell into a trance. He saw heaven opened and something like a large sheet being let down to earth by its four corners. It contained all kinds of four-footed animals, as well as reptiles and birds. Then a voice told him, "Get up, Peter. Kill and eat."

"Surely not, Lord!" Peter replied. "I have never eaten anything impure or unclean."

The voice spoke to him a second time, "Do not call anything impure that God has made clean."

This happened three times, and immediately the sheet was taken back to heaven.

While Peter was wondering about the meaning of the vision, the men sent by Cornelius found out where Simon's house was and stopped at the gate. They called out, asking if Simon who was known as Peter was staying there.

While Peter was still thinking about the vision, the Spirit said to him, "Simon, three men are looking for you. So get up and go downstairs. Do not hesitate to go with them, for I have sent them."

Peter went down and said to the men, "I'm the one you're looking for. Why have you come?"

The men replied, "We have come from Cornelius the centurion. He is a righteous and God-fearing man, who is respected by all the Jewish people. A holy angel told him to ask you to come to his house so that he could hear what you have to say." Then Peter invited the men into the house to be his guests.

The next day Peter started out with them, and some of the believers from Joppa went along. The following day he arrived in Caesarea. Cornelius was expecting them and had called together his relatives and close friends. As Peter entered the house, Cornelius met him and fell at his feet in reverence. But Peter made him get up. "Stand up," he said, "I am only a man myself."

While talking with him, Peter went inside and found a large gathering of people. He said to them: "You are well aware that it is against our law for a Jew to associate with or visit a Gentile. But God has shown me that I should not call anyone impure or unclean."

Peter went on to say he realized that God doesn't show favoritism but invites people from every ethnic group and nation to accept the gospel through Jesus the Messiah. As Peter was explaining the gospel message and the first-ever Gentile audience was responding with faith and repentance, something amazing happened: the gift of the Holy Spirit was poured out on them just as it had been on the Jewish believers on the day of Pentecost.

At the same time the church was growing, it was also facing persecution from Herod Agrippa I, the grandson of Herod the Great (who reigned when Jesus was born) and nephew of Herod Antipas (who had John the Baptist beheaded).

It was about this time that King Herod arrested some who belonged to the church, intending to persecute them. He had James, the brother of John, put to death with the sword. When he saw that this met with approval among the Jews, he proceeded to seize Peter also. This happened during the Festival of Unleavened Bread. After arresting him, he put him in prison, handing him over to be guarded by four squads of four soldiers each. Herod intended to bring him out for public trial after the Passover.

So Peter was kept in prison, but the church was earnestly praying to God for him.

The night before Herod was to bring him to trial, Peter was sleeping between two soldiers, bound with two chains, and sentries stood guard at the entrance. Suddenly an angel of the Lord appeared and a light shone in the cell. He struck Peter on the side and woke him up. "Quick, get up!" he said, and the chains fell off Peter's wrists.

Then the angel said to him, "Put on your clothes and sandals." And Peter did so. "Wrap your cloak around you and follow me," the angel told him. Peter followed him out of the prison, but he had no idea that what the angel was doing was really happening; he thought he was seeing a vision. They passed the first and second guards and came to the iron gate leading to the city. It opened for them by itself, and they went through it. When they had walked the length of one street, suddenly the angel left him.

Then Peter came to himself and said, "Now I know without a doubt that the Lord has sent his angel and rescued me from Herod's clutches and from everything the Jewish people were hoping would happen."

When this had dawned on him, he went to the house of Mary the mother of John, also called Mark, where many people had gathered and were praying. Peter knocked at the outer entrance, and a servant named Rhoda came to answer the door. When she recognized Peter's voice, she was so overjoyed she ran back without opening it and exclaimed, "Peter is at the door!"

"You're out of your mind," they told her. When she kept insisting that it was so, they said, "It must be his angel."

But Peter kept on knocking, and when they opened the door and saw him, they were astonished. Peter motioned with his hand for them to be quiet and described how the Lord had brought him out of prison. "Tell James and the other brothers and sisters about this," he said, and then he left for another place.

In the morning, there was no small commotion among the soldiers as to what had become of Peter. After Herod had a thorough search made for him and did not find him, he cross-examined the guards and ordered that they be executed.

Then Herod went from Judea to Caesarea and stayed there. He had been quarreling with the people of Tyre and Sidon; they now joined together and sought an audience with him. After securing the support of Blastus, a trusted personal servant of the king, they asked for peace, because they depended on the king's country for their food supply.

On the appointed day Herod, wearing his royal robes, sat on his throne and delivered a public address to the people. They shouted, "This is the voice of a god, not of a man." Immediately, because Herod did not give praise to God, an angel of the Lord struck him down, and he was eaten by worms and died.

But the word of God continued to spread and flourish.

Saul and his mentor Barnabas spent a year ministering to the first largely Gentile church at Antioch, where the believers were first called "Christians." From there the Lord called them to missionary service. Saul and Barnabas, accompanied at first by John Mark— who was Barnabas's cousin and who would later write the Gospel of Mark—began traveling and proclaiming Jesus throughout Asia Minor. It was also during this time that Saul got a name change to "Paul." Because God's Spirit was leading them, Saul (Paul) and his colleagues boldly spoke about Jesus everywhere they went. Little did they know what they would have to endure for the Good News.

—Includes portions of Acts 1–10, 12

Participant's Guide

Introduction

"It's nice to share our toys!" That's what parents in every generation tell their little children. Some kids get the message and others don't seem to catch on.

Teenagers face the same challenge. "Let someone else use the remote control and pick the TV show." "Don't grab the last piece of pizza."

Fortunately, people become generous and share naturally by the time they enter the grown-up world ... right? Wrong! It is still a battle and a challenge, well into our adult years.

In this episode of *The Story* we hear our heavenly Father say, "It's nice to share!" God tells his people that the grace they have received, the love they are experiencing, the amazing fellowship they share as a community of believers, the forgiveness of sins, and the restored relationship they have with God should not be hoarded and kept hidden. God calls his people, then and now, to share the good news and hope found in Jesus alone.

How are we doing? Are we quick to share? Have we discovered that the more we give away the things of God, the more we have?

Talk About It

Describe a time when you had something brand new and found it difficult to share with others.

Video Teaching Notes

As you watch the video segment for session 7, use the following outline to record anything that stands out to you.

I. From creation to the resurrection ... God's plan to restore us

II. The presence and power of the Holy Spirit

III. Revival and the birth of a new community

IV. What the early believers did when they gathered

Video Discussion

1. In the video segment, Randy gave a snapshot of the gospel and reminded us that if we believe that Jesus was God among us, lived a sinless life, died for our sins, and rose again, we can become children of God. How did you learn this truth and who did God use to share it with you?

2. Jesus was clear that our source of power to share his life-saving message is the Holy Spirit (Acts 1:8). Indeed, the people experienced this when the Spirit came on them (Acts 2:1 – 4); likewise, Peter was filled with the Spirit and proclaimed the message with boldness (Acts 2:14 – 40; all references included in the session's Bible Reading). How have you experienced the Holy Spirit filling you, moving you, and giving you strength to share the message and love of Jesus?

> *The Spirit is going to dwell in the lives of all believers in Jesus. His presence will give the disciples the courage, guidance, and power to pull off their new mission.*

3. Jesus told his followers that their ministry would occur in four distinct locations (Acts 1:8; included in the session's Bible Reading). How do you see God using you, your church, and the church at large to share the life-saving message of Jesus in each of the following places:

• Jerusalem (your hometown/neighborhood)

• Judea (your surrounding community and region)

• Samaria (the tough places that many people avoid)

• The ends of the earth (around the nation and world)

How could your group members team up to get involved in sharing the love, grace, and message of Jesus in one of these places?

4. Along with sharing the message and love of Jesus, we are also called to share our resources/material goods, our meals/fellowship, and our lives/stories. How is each valuable and what can we do to share these more intentionally?

> *Out of the overflow of their lives together, they began to meet the needs of each other and the people around them. Their offer of care was different. It was unconditional.*

5. What sorts of conflict and spiritual battle did the early Christians face as they tried to share Jesus' message? How did they respond to persecution and resistance and how can this inspire us as we encounter people who push back against the message of God's love?

6. Peter (Acts 4:8 – 12), Stephen (Acts 6:8 – 15; 7:51 – 60; all references included in the session's Bible Reading), and later the apostle Paul were clear that Jesus Christ was the Messiah, the only hope for salvation. How did people respond to that bold claim in the religiously diverse ancient world and how do they respond today? How do we continue sharing with boldness, even when others disagree with us?

7. Three thousand people came to faith in Jesus at Pentecost and their ranks swelled in succeeding days. Is your local church seeing regular conversions and lives changed by Jesus? If so, how can you celebrate and encourage this? If not, what steps can you take to help your church reach out more effectively with the life-saving love and message of Jesus?

8. The risen Jesus called his followers to be his witnesses. Give an example of how we can share the message of the gospel in one of the following ways:

- By sharing the story of Jesus

- By sharing the story of when we placed our faith in the Savior

- By sharing specific stories about the presence and power of Jesus at work in our life today

> *Jesus told us over and over again that if we will acknowledge him for who he is and will acknowledge our sin and accept his gift as full payment we can become children of God. This is called "the gospel" or "the good news."*

Closing Prayer

As you take time to pray, here are some ideas to get you started:

- Pray for boldness and clarity as you share the good news of Jesus with others.

- Ask for God to help you grow in generosity as you learn to share the resources he has put in your care.

- Pray for God to build your small group into a place where real community and grace are extended freely.

In the Coming Days

Personal Reflections

Reflect this week on the people who shared the gospel of Jesus with you. What did they say? How did their lives reinforce the message of God's great love? Seek to use their examples as inspiration as you share the grace and the good news of Jesus with those you encounter each day.

Personal Action

The early Christians loved to open their homes for meals with others. In the coming weeks, make two invitations. First, invite a few Christians over for a meal and a time of sharing life and faith. Second, invite a few people you care about who are not yet followers of Jesus and have them share a meal with you and some of your Christian friends.

The Story, NIV

The Bible as One Continuing Story of God and His People

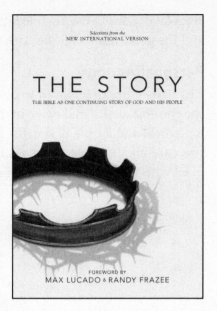

"THE GREATEST STORY EVER TOLD" IS MORE THAN JUST A CLICHÉ. God goes to great lengths to rescue lost and hurting people. That is what *The Story* is all about: the story of the Bible, God's great love affair with humanity. Condensed into 31 accessible chapters, *The Story* sweeps you into the unfolding progression of Bible characters and events from Genesis to Revelation.

Using the clear, accessible text of the NIV Bible, it allows the stories, poems, and teachings of the Bible to read like a novel. And like any good story, *The Story* is filled with intrigue, drama, conflict, romance, and redemption; and this story's true!

Features: • The story of the Bible—in its own words. Selections from the NIV Bible with short transitions to connect the reader to the continuing story. • Events, characters, and teachings of the Bible arranged chronologically • Timelines of Bible events • New International Version (NIV) Bible text Learn more about this whole-church experience at TheStory.com.

The Story Adult Curriculum

Getting to the Heart of God's Story

Randy Frazee

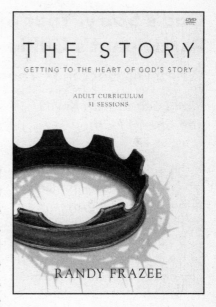

To understand the Bible, says author and pastor Randy Frazee, you need bifocal lenses, because two perspectives are involved. The Lower Story, our story, is actually many stories of men and women interacting with God in the daily course of life. The Upper Story is God's story, the tale of his great, overarching purpose that fits all the individual stories together like panels in one unified mural. Bestselling author Max Lucado also adds some introductory insights.

Through these 31 video sessions, *The Story* DVD curriculum will open your eyes to God's master-plan as it unfolds in the lives of the Bible's characters. Discover the heart of God's Upper Story and the joy that comes as you align your story with God's. The *Story* DVD and Participant's Guide (sold separately) are designed for use by groups of all sizes, including small groups and Sunday school and adult education classes, for each of the 31 weeks of *The Story* church-wide journey.

Available in stores and online!

God's Story, Your Story Participant's Guide

When His Becomes Yours

Max Lucado with Kevin and Sherry Harney

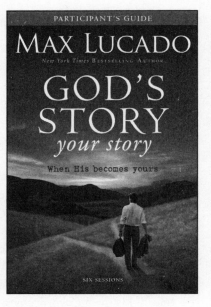

In this six-session study (video sold separately), popular pastor and bestselling author Max Lucado gives you a fresh perspective on how your daily life relates to God's grand, epic story. Your journey of faith will come alive as you explore the divine narrative in New Testament and contemporary characters, and discover how the ancient stories of Scripture reveal God's plans for you today.

Join America's favorite Christian author for a personal look at the story of God's eternal redemption being told through your individual story right now.

Available in stores and online!

Walking with God in the Desert Discovery Guide

Seven Faith Lessons

Ray Vander Laan with Stephen and Amanda Sorenson

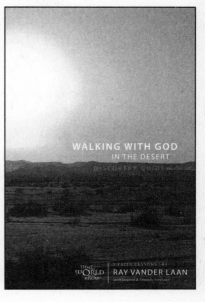

Filmed on location in the Middle East, Faith Lessons is a unique series (video sold separately) that brings God's Word to life with astounding relevance. By weaving together the Bible's fascinating historical, cultural, religious, and geo-graphical contexts, teacher and historian Ray Vander Laan reveals keen insights into the Scriptures' significance for modern believers. The Faith Lessons series is ideal for churches, small groups, families, and individuals. Discovery Guides feature five days of personal study for each lesson.

The seven sessions in this particular volume are:

1. Join the Journey
2. It's Hot in Here and There's No Way Out
3. Help Is Here
4. When Your Heart Cries Out
5. They Were Not Wandering
6. Ears to Hear
7. There's Hope in the Desert

Available in stores and online!

When God's Spirit Moves Participant's Guide

Six Sessions on the Life-Changing Power of the Holy Spirit

Jim Cymbala with Dean Merrill

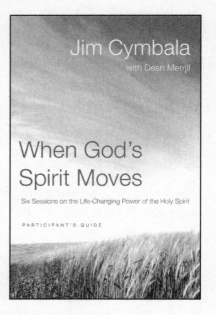

What happens when the Holy Spirit moves in a church? In this six-session study with video sold separately, you'll not only learn about the person of the Holy Spirit, you'll learn:

- How to make room for the work of the Spirit in your life and in your church
- How the Spirit empowers you to be creative and honor God with your gifts and talents
- How to listen in prayer and apply the Word of God
- How the Spirit is active in the work of healing your body, your emotions, and your relationships
- How your personal transformation leads to grater transformations in your community and around the world through the changed lives of believers
- How your church can become a place where the message of the gospel is heard and people experience the life-giving power of a grace-filled community

Pastor and bestselling author Jim Cymbala will show you how to infuse a fresh sense of God's power in your church and in your life as a follower of Jesus.

Available in stores and online!

Zondervan Small Group Bible Study YouTube Playlist

Watch Over 100 Full Bible Study Sessions for Free

Watch the entire first lesson for many of Zondervan's DVD based Bible studies. No more guessing on the content, instead you get the full video experience by being able to see and evaluate the complete first lesson of each multi-lesson Bible study.

Each video is easy to share with your friends, small group or Bible study. Just hit the 'share' button under the video and send it via email, Facebook, or Twitter.

Watch Bible study sessions from bestselling authors like Timothy Keller, Andy Stanley, Anne Graham Lotz , Bill Hybels, Craig Groeschel, Jim Cymbala, John Ortberg, Lysa TerKeurst , and many more.

Zondervan video-based group Bible studies are available on DVD, and many are available for download. These video Bible studies feature a variety of topics from many authors, and are available wherever small group resources and curriculum are sold.

Watch sessions from bestselling studies including:

* *The Reason for God* by Timothy Keller
* *Guardrails* by Andy Stanley
* *The Christian Atheist* by Craig Groeschel
* *Undaunted* by Christine Caine
* *The Circle Maker* by Mark Batterson

Available in stores and online!

Share Your Thoughts

With the Author: Your comments will be forwarded to the author when you send them to *zauthor@zondervan.com*.

With Zondervan: Submit your review of this book by writing to *zreview@zondervan.com*.

Free Online Resources at
www.zondervan.com

Zondervan AuthorTracker: Be notified whenever your favorite authors publish new books, go on tour, or post an update about what's happening in their lives at www.zondervan.com/authortracker.

Daily Bible Verses and Devotions: Enrich your life with daily Bible verses or devotions that help you start every morning focused on God. Visit www.zondervan.com/newsletters.

Free Email Publications: Sign up for newsletters on Christian living, academic resources, church ministry, fiction, children's resources, and more. Visit www.zondervan.com/newsletters.

Zondervan Bible Search: Find and compare Bible passages in a variety of translations at www.zondervanbiblesearch.com.

Other Benefits: Register to receive online benefits like coupons and special offers, or to participate in research.

ZONDERVAN

ZONDERVAN.com/
AUTHORTRACKER
follow your favorite authors